## PRAISE FOR *RIDE NORTH*

'I loved this: funny, quirky, exciting and moving. Folly and Tooth are a great double-act. If you're a horse person you'll adore it; if you're not a horse person, it'll turn you into one'
ANTHONY MCGOWAN

'*Ride North* is a quirky adventure with a distinctive voice that explores grief, family, love and connection, especially with friends of the four-legged variety'
FRANCES MOLONEY

'A poignant and tender story of love, loss, friendship and hope. Tooth is quite possibly the most engaging "talking pony" I've ever encountered in fiction. The ending was perfect – made me laugh and cry simultaneously'
TANYA LANDMAN

'A powerful, wise and gripping story from a wonderful new voice in children's literature. *Ride North* is a beautiful tale of love, courage and the unique bond between a girl and her horse. It deserves a place alongside the classic horse and pony stories'
ANNELISE GRAY

'Maria de Jong weaves a beautiful tale of adventure, survival and hope, exploring the deep bond between a girl and her pony. With vivid prose that brings every scene to life, de Jong makes the reader feel they're right there alongside Folly and Tooth on their exhilarating, sometimes perilous journey. Through evocative descriptions and compelling narrative, balancing humour, sadness and wonder, de Jong's skilful storytelling creates a rich, unforgettable experience'

J. P. Rose

'Maria de Jong's gorgeously lyrical debut is wry, funny and at times heart-achingly sad. Folly is an engaging young hero: gnarly and determined to ride north with beloved horse Tooth to Cape Rēinga, where Tasman Sea meets Pacific Ocean. Their unique bond allows them to outwit pursuers and overcome obstacles on a vividly painted journey through the beautiful New Zealand landscape'

Gita Ralleigh

'A surreal, poignant and punchy MG novel, that lovers of adventure, horses and family dramas will devour. The magical elements – occasional sightings of her mother's ghost, and in particular her relationship with Tooth, who is ally, mentor and wise counsel – are really well done. Tooth brings heaps of humour and warmth to the book. I love the adventure and the magic, but in the end it's the emotional heart and punch and – no spoilers – family resolution, that lift this great MG adventure'

Chris Vick

# RIDE NORTH

First published in Great Britain in 2025 by
Andersen Press Limited
20 Vauxhall Bridge Road, London SW1V 2SA, UK
Vijverlaan 48, 3062 HL Rotterdam, Nederland
www.andersenpress.co.uk

2 4 6 8 10 9 7 5 3 1



British Library Cataloguing in Publication Data available.

ISBN 978 1 83913 520 0

Printed and bound in Great Britain by Clays Ltd, Elcograf S.p.A.

# RIDE NORTH

MARIA DE JONG

ANDERSEN PRESS

*In Māori culture, Cape Rēinga is a sacred site where spirits take their final leave from the world of the living. It is not a cemetery or a place to scatter human ashes.*

*This is a made-up story. Any similarity to actual events or to horses or people you may know is pure chance.*

*For Mum, who loved children and books.*
*For Dad, who took me to the horses.*
*For Mauro, who said, 'Dream on!'*
*and meant it the right way.*

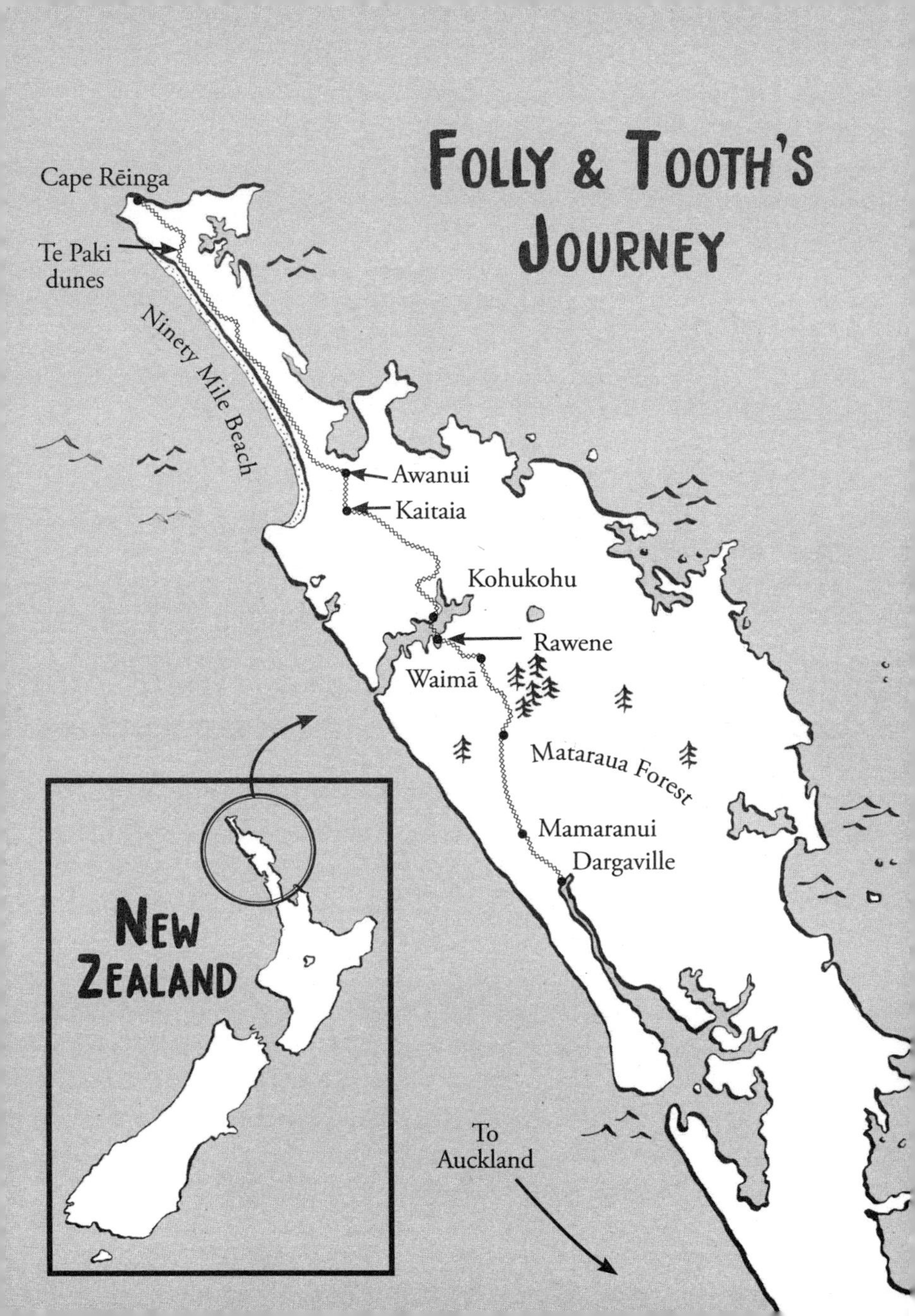
Folly & Tooth's Journey
Cape Rēinga
Te Paki dunes
Ninety Mile Beach
Awanui
Kaitaia
Kohukohu
Rawene
Waimā
Mataraua Forest
Mamaranui
Dargaville
To Auckland
New Zealand

# 1

It was my first time skipping school, and even though I'd biked to Tooth's paddock a million times before, it felt strange to be going there so early on a weekday. Down at the river road I hid behind a bush, changed out of my uniform and stuffed it into my backpack. I didn't want some nosy grown-up asking why I wasn't in class.

The Wairoa was still churned up after the bad weather, shining like a pinky-brown highway in the morning sun. Ducks rode fast on the current. A skiff that had broken its mooring bobbed along with them.

I had everything figured out. Once I reached the paddock the only thing left to do was sort the gear. Tooth would grumble again about having to carry it, I'd promise him extra oats and we'd be on our way. Easy.

That truck driver must have been flooring it. The engine noise shook the air. I glanced back and saw a metal grille coming at me like bared teeth, and as I did, my front wheel hit a pothole. The bike wobbled. The truck clipped the back wheel and then for the strangest moment everything warped: I was fast-floating and the bike was slow-bouncing and somewhere a dog was yowling like a sick violin.

I hit the ground. The truck roared off. The road was empty. No one saw a thing.

# 2

I woke staring up Tooth's left nostril, his whiskers tickling my face.

'You look terrible, what happened?'

'A truck hit me.' I sat up, woozy. 'How did I get here?'

'Walked. I whinnied but you didn't notice. And you forgot to close the gate.'

I groaned. The truck . . . the mangled bike lying beside me on the river bank . . . it all came back. I could have been killed! A memory of my own plodding footsteps flashed through my head. I'd been in shock. The same part of my brain that had set me on autopilot to the paddock must have told me the shelter would be a good place to rest.

I groaned again. Tooth gave me a friendly nudge, shying

away at my '*Ow!*' of pain. My arm throbbed where I'd landed on it. When I pulled up my T-shirt sleeve there was a dark swirly bruise, though amazingly nothing seemed broken.

'Impressive.' He drew closer again for a better look. 'So it's off, then.'

'What's off?'

'The trip.'

I knew I'd been forgetting something.

'No!' I clambered to my feet. 'We're going!'

He snorted. 'My big mouth. To be honest, you don't look up to much.'

'I'm fine.' Truth was I felt awful, but making it to the paddock after getting sideswiped by a truck seemed like a sign that the trip was meant to be.

Tooth gave me an 'Oh?' look and worked his jaw, considering.

'All right,' he said at last, 'but I want a decent feed first. Call me when you're ready.' He ambled off to graze.

I had to do most of the packing one-handed because my arm hurt, so the backpack came out pretty lumpy, but everything fit. The pop-up tent was a problem. Tooth and I had to look normal. Who took a neon-green pancake bag on an ordinary afternoon ride? In the end I rolled it up, rammed it down one side of the pack and covered the part poking out with a T-shirt. Not great, but better.

Tooth trotted back over when I whistled. I gave him a carrot and a peppermint to put him in a good mood, then brushed and saddled him.

'Cushy,' he said when I'd arranged the sleeping bag under the saddle blanket. I went over his hooves one last time before mounting. 'You did that yesterday,' he pointed out. I checked them anyway. A lame pony would ruin everything.

My arm screamed when I slung the backpack on, but it was better once I had it in position. I climbed into the saddle from the fence.

'Well, here goes.'

Tooth was playing it cool, but I could tell he was eager too. He didn't complain about the load and there was a spring in his step as we left the paddock. It was pretty quiet on the road, mostly farm trucks, a car or two, one tour bus. Things would really get going when the holidaymakers started heading north next day. By then we planned to be in the back country.

My heart was fluttering. We were on our way! When we came to a wide stretch, Tooth broke into a canter without a touch from me. As his hooves drummed the grass verge I gave a whoop of joy. He put on a final burst, then slowed back down to a jog.

'This pad thing's hot,' he said, meaning the sleeping bag. 'My back's sweating already.'

'I'll take it off at the dirt road.'

Soon the bungalows and lawn pools and double carports became farm country where the fence lines disappeared into the hills and a smell of hay mixed in with the heat. The land seemed to stretch out properly and breathe. There were cows, sheep, horses – even deer. Through Tooth's pricked ears the road unwound ahead as simple as the line I'd drawn on the map tucked in my pack.

'See – told you it wasn't hard,' I said, swinging my legs and feeling smug.

He blew through his nose. 'My hooves will decide that.'

We passed a farmhouse with a car just like Dad's parked in the driveway.

'What do you think he'll do when he figures out I'm gone?'

'Call the police. And when they see *I'm* missing they'll put two and two together and start looking for a girl on a horse. Trust me – you'll be sleeping in your own bed tonight.'

I stuck my chin out. 'No I won't.' Who would notice his empty paddock? It was back from the road and hidden by a belt of trees. Apart from Dad, who'd dropped by in winter to bring hay bales, the last people I'd seen go near it had been some council workers marking land boundaries. That had been weeks ago. Tooth was wrong. We were going to do this thing. We had the map and the pop-up and easily enough supplies. 'Best Food,' I said quickly, before he could bring down the mood. It was a game we had, telling each other our best this or that.

'Stud farm oats,' he answered after a moment. 'Stolen.'

'Huh?'

Before he came to Dargaville Tooth was a track pony on a stud farm. Track ponies calm the racehorses down. The grazing had been great, but overall he hadn't enjoyed his time there much. Thoroughbreds can be uppity.

'All the horses on the farm except me were on fancy training diets. Oats, corn, barley, molasses – you name it. Always bragging about who had the best deal. It got so I had to even things up.'

'How?'

He whinny-chuckled. 'I figured out how to open the catch on the feed room door. It drove those blowhards crazy. "You don't earn it like we do,"' he said, mimicking a whiny racehorse. 'I got fatter than a summer tick.'

'Did the owner ever find out?'

He nodded. 'Caught me with my face in a feed bin. I did time in starvation.'

'What's that?'

'A paddock that cows are grazing out. Imagine: me, with cows!'

'What's wrong with cows?'

'They fart.'

'So do you!'

'Not like a cow.'

Secretly I was thinking the stud farm had left him with some uppity ideas of his own, but all I said was, 'Chips are my

BF today.' I didn't mention the fish that went with them. Tooth thinks eating other animals is gross.

Even though I didn't let on, his words about the police had set me worrying. We had to leave the main road.

'Come on, let's get moving.'

I urged him into a trot.

# 3

Tooth's his own boss. I take care of him and in exchange he lets me ride him. He isn't much to look at, just a nuggety little bay with a longish face and a white dab on his forehead. The dab is why I call him Tooth. He's OK with that. Says I couldn't get my tongue around his real name in a million years.

'Try me,' I say, and his nostrils quiver like he's about to laugh.

Before he came along I used to ride at a place called Novaks' outside town. The mounts stood saddled up, looking bored, and I was so horse-starved I thought they were terrific: Roly the nippy Shetland, 'Sharkeye' Amy, Hank the Tank, sway-backed old Jake and Minecraft, a hard-mouthed piebald Mrs Novak's son usually belted around on.

‘Oh, Mirko can ride anything,’ Mrs Novak would tell people, and even though Mirko was a pimply show-off who laughed like a honking goose, I was still jealous, because more than anything I wanted someone to say that about me.

The first time I got on Tooth I was so nervous I made every mistake in the book. He put up with it until we were out of earshot of Mum and Dad, who’d come to the paddock to watch, and then told me plain as day, ‘Stop doing that.’

I pulled up. ‘Doing what?’

‘That twitchy thing with the reins. It’s confusing.’

‘Oh. Sorry.’

I wasn’t surprised he was communicating with me. The horses at Novaks’ never had, except in the usual ways horses show their moods, but why should they? I was just another clumsy beginner in an endless stream.

‘You probably weren’t listening,’ Tooth had said later. ‘Most people don’t, you know.’

Maybe. All I knew was that with Tooth it was different.

He was my dream pony. I loved him the minute I saw him and I wanted him to love me back. Of course we understood each other.

His version was less gushy. 'It made sense to get along,' he'd say.

Over the weeks and months he slowly undid my bad habits.

'Sit deeper.'

'Use your leg muscles.'

'Don't throw your weight about.'

It was easier to see what he meant without a saddle and stirrups, so I rode bareback until I'd more or less gotten the hang of it.

I pestered him. I might not have had proper riding lessons but I'd read plenty. 'Are my hands light? Is my seat good? Should we try lunging to lengthen your stride?' He'd just roll his eyes.

'You'll do,' he finally told me one day, probably sick and

tired of all the questions. I think he meant I'd finally learned some respect.

Tooth's other name may be a mouthful, but mine was a mistake. It took a long time for me to be born and Mum told me that by the end of it Dad was so shellshocked he could hardly say his own name right, let alone make sure mine got registered properly. Folly Crewe: once the damage was done my parents decided they liked it that way and left it.

'Pinch of her dippy mum,' reckoned Dad.

'Touch of her goofy dad,' chuckled Mum.

Was I meant to be Holly or Polly or what? They never said.

Mum died a year and a half ago. Not long afterwards Dad met Audrey at a garage sale and they started going out. Easy as pie. Dad sat me and my little brother Dylan down and told us how Mum's illness had left him drained and lonely and that meeting Audrey had given him another shot at life. He said once we got to know her we'd like her as much as he did. That same night I took out my pocket knife and made Dylan swear in blood that we'd never, ever let her be a part of our family.

Audrey had this thing about being there when Dylan and I came home from school each day, 'to welcome us' – like it was her place, not ours. She was always wiping the bench, plumping the sofa cushions, that sort of thing. She baked, too, which is something Mum hardly ever did. I tried to make Dylan promise he wouldn't eat any of her stuff, but the first batch of double chocolate muffins broke him. I don't really blame him, he's only six.

One day when I walked into the kitchen, Dylan was feeding fresh-baked lemon cake to his Chewbacca action figure. Audrey was reading something on her laptop.

'Hi, Folly. School OK?' she asked, all casual on purpose. She was always like that – too friendly, too bakey, too everything.

'Amazing.'

She flashed me one of her try-hard smiles. 'Something fun happen?'

'Yeah, Jayden Wright shot a snot rocket into Emily Maxwell's lunchbox.'

Dylan snorted on his milk and sprayed Audrey's laptop. While she flapped about for a cloth I slipped past and went up to my room.

# 4

Someone knocked.

'Who is it?'

'Me.'

I opened the door. Dylan climbed straight onto my bed and propped Chewbacca up beside him.

'She says do you want cake.'

'No. And you said you wouldn't eat her stuff.'

'I was starving.'

Dylan loves food. He's an easy target for Audrey. He wiped the crumbs off his lips and sat there staring at the horse pictures I'd stuck all over the wall.

'That's new, where'd you get it?' He pointed at a rearing Arabian stallion.

I'd cut it out of a library book and felt guilty ever since. Still, not putting it up would have been worse.

'A witch gave it to me.'

Dylan pouted. 'No such thing as witches.'

'Shows how much you know. There's one in our kitchen right now.'

'That's just Audrey.'

'Just Audrey' – she was getting to him. I love Dylan, but he's too soft for war. Soon he'd be crawling into her lap for bedtime stories.

'Dylan,' I said carefully, 'have you ever seen Mum since . . . well, you know?'

I didn't want to start him off crying, but it was something I had to find out. Because I had. Seen her ghost, I mean. Not the woo-woo kind – more a quick shimmer and then gone. The shimmer had a pleading look. Maybe Dylan knew what I meant.

He stared at me with his wide eyes. He got those from Mum. The dark wavy hair, too. I ended up with Dad's sandy colouring.

'Uh-huh,' he nodded, all serious. 'I dreamed she gave me a stun gun like Kyle's, only better.'

Kyle lives next door.

'Not in a dream. I mean for real.'

'Course not,' he said. 'They made her into dust.' He slid off the bed. 'Chewie's still hungry. We're going back down to the kitchen.'

'Tell the witch lemon cake gives me a rash.'

I didn't slash Audrey's tyres or anything; instead I wore her down with the small stuff. I knew it got to her. She wanted Dad to think she could handle me, but I could tell deep down she was itching to go ballistic.

'Eating here must save you a ton on groceries,' I said to her that night when Dad had left the dinner table to take a call. I jabbed a potato onto my fork. 'Bet your bank account's heaving.'

Audrey's mouth tightened but she said nothing. When she asked me to help clear the table I rolled my eyes so only she could see. Later, we were alone in the kitchen and I kept up the pressure.

'Homework all done?' she asked.

'Homework all done? Homework all done?' I parroted, and walked out.

At bedtime, after she'd left, Dad looked in on me.

'Mind if I come in?'

That was Dadspeak for 'time to talk'. I pretended to keep reading.

He sat down on the edge of the bed. 'Good book?'

'Uh-huh.' I turned the page and fake-read some more.

Dad looked at the walls. He stared at the library-book stallion. For one terrible moment I thought he knew the truth, until he cleared his throat in a where-do-I-begin sort of way and said, 'Sweetheart, what's eating you?'

My throat tightened. Ever since Mum's death a knot of feelings had been growing inside me. But before I could start to untangle them he went on.

'You've been pretty unwelcoming towards Audrey since . . . well, ever since you met her, actually,' he said. 'I know things happened quickly after your mum—'

'I've seen her!' I blurted.

Dad looked puzzled. 'Who?'

'Mum!' And then I told him about the shimmers. When I'd finished I sneaked a look at his face. I was afraid he'd think I was making it up, or just plain crazy.

'It's because she's worried about us,' I said in a rush, to get him on the right track. 'She can see how sad we are about the way things are going and she wants to help but she can't because there are people in the house who don't belong. She needs more time. We haven't even buried her ashes yet!'

It was true. How could Mum's spirit ever be at peace without a proper resting place?

'If it was just you and me and Dylan again maybe she could tell us what's wrong.' I had to make him understand.

Dad was quiet for a moment. He raked his fingers through the thinning top part of his hair and gave a deep sigh. Then, in his special Patient Dad voice he said, 'Folly, do you remember when you found Tooth?'

What a question – how could I forget? I'd seen him grazing on a grass verge when I was biking home from school one day. He'd escaped from a nearby farm. I'd taken the uneaten carrot out of my lunchbox and walked straight up to him. It never crossed my mind that he wouldn't want to be my friend. Tooth says for him the carrot swung it.

'And you remember what happened when you found out he was for sale?'

I nodded again. I had begged Mum and Dad to buy him.

When they'd said no, too expensive, no place to put him, what about all the vet bills, I'd gone on a hunger strike.

'We told you the time wasn't right,' Dad went on, 'but that maybe in a few years, once we'd paid off the house, you could find another horse to buy. And what did you say?'

I flashed him a wary glance. Where was this leading?

'You told us you only wanted Tooth,' Dad reminded me. 'That he was the right horse for you – the only one – and that he wouldn't be there in a few years.'

'So?' I was definitely suspicious now.

'So that's the way I feel about Audrey,' Dad said. 'Maybe she came along a bit too soon, but I know she's the right person for me.'

He'd trapped me.

'But you can wait! It doesn't have to be now, before we've even . . .' The words choked in my throat.

Dad put a hand on my arm and said gently, 'Life doesn't

wait, Folly. I loved your mother so very, very much . . . but she's gone, and I don't want to be alone. I'd be miserable company for you and Dylan.' He paused and looked at the stallion again for a moment without really seeing it, then went on. 'I was going to wait and tell you both together, but maybe it's better this way. You can help Dylan get used to the idea.' He cleared his throat again. 'There'll be some changes in the next months. I've been promoted.'

What did his job have to do with anything? I tried to sound pleased, but I was confused.

'That's great, Dad. Are you Murray's boss now?'

'I won't be working with Murray any more. The job's in Auckland.' Before what he was saying had even begun to sink in, he ploughed on. 'The lease on Audrey's flat will be running out soon and I . . . *we've* decided to find a place together. All four of us. The timing's perfect. If we move after Christmas you and Dylan can settle in and still enjoy the summer before school cranks up again in February.'

Move to Auckland? My stomach lurched. But Dad looked really excited.

'It might seem a bit strange and sudden at first, but trust me, this is the right move.' When I said nothing he gave me a hug. Maybe he thought my silence meant I was OK with the whole thing. 'It'll be good, Folly, you'll see. Things have been tough . . .' He looked at me and added gently, '. . . for you too with your school friends, right?'

I looked away. Since Mum's funeral I'd been so twisted up inside I was no fun to be around. The kids at school pretty much left me alone – even my best friend had found a new best friend. I spent most of my time on my own or with Tooth.

'This will be a new beginning for all of us,' Dad carried on. 'We'll be a real family again.'

I finally found the voice to squawk, 'What about Tooth?'

'There probably won't be any paddocks close by the new house – Auckland's a proper city! But there are pony clubs where he can stay. You might not be able to ride every day like now, but Tooth will be just fine.'

Tooth and I had been to a pony club open day once. All the kids had been wearing breeches and riding boots and their horses had perfectly braided manes. I was in jeans and gumboots. Tooth's mane doesn't braid. We'd never gone back.

All at once it clicked that Dad and Audrey had already decided everything behind my back; even if I said no, it was settled. Maybe Audrey had faked the whole flat lease thing and Dad had fallen for it. She'd won. In her mind she was probably popping the bubbly twenty-four-seven.

Dad went on talking over my silence. House this, garden that . . . big school . . . good ratings . . . new friends . . . My face felt like granite. I didn't care about any dumb new house. I didn't want a school with a million strangers.

'It's a lot to take on board at once,' Dad said. 'But I know you'll do great. We all will.' He kissed me goodnight, switched off my reading lamp and got up to go. At the door he turned.

'Let's do something special this weekend to celebrate – all four of us. Maybe go to that new slippery slide place and then pizza. What do you say?'

I mumbled some kind of answer. Dad was so blinded by the promotion and Audrey's moves that he was rushing headlong into a huge mistake! Why couldn't he see it?

When he'd gone I turned the light back on. There was a framed photo on the bedside table. In it Mum and I were standing on the footpath outside a shop. It was a windy day and we were both laughing and trying to keep the hair out of our faces as she snapped us on her phone. Her hair was as straight and straw-coloured as mine – in the shop she'd plunked the wig on over what was left of her own dark locks and hugged me close as we looked at ourselves in the mirror. 'See – twins,' she'd said to the assistant. 'We'll take this one too.' She had worn it home.

'Woah, double trouble,' Dad had joked when he'd seen us. Then, seeing Mum's smile wobble, he'd pulled her into his arms.

I missed Mum so bad. 'I won't get used to it,' I promised out loud. No way was I going on any slippery slide 'fun' day with Audrey and no *way* was I going to Auckland. I switched the light off and lay staring at the ceiling in the dark, thinking up a plan.

# 5

Next day at school we were doing geography and the teacher was talking about how the Tasman Sea and the Pacific Ocean come together above the tip of the North Island. Mrs Pukeroa's proud of her Māori roots, so she told us about Cape Rēinga being the special place where souls move from this world into the next.

I was telling Tooth about it later when the idea hit me.

'That's it! We can take Mum's ashes there!' Dad had put the cylinder that held them in the lounge cabinet. It would be easy to get.

Tooth and I are both twelve, but he's been around more than me. He doesn't like to rush things.

'How far?' he asked.

‘Like Uncle Dan’s place times eight. See?’ I held up my phone to show him. ‘It’ll be much better than some old cemetery – Mum loved the sea.’ My imagination was flying. I could already smell the salt air.

‘What about nights?’

‘Beach pop-up, sleeping bag. And a map and a torch and water bottles and the folding bucket and cans of food.’ The ideas came tumbling out.

‘Do I look like a pack mule to you?’

Tooth might grizzle, but I knew he’d come through for me. Besides, I had my own ways to soften him up.

‘It won’t weigh much. And we don’t need cooking stuff – I’ll buy takeaways with my birthday money. You can have chips.’

‘OK, but without the slime.’

‘It’s called tomato sauce.’

That’s how everything started. Now I know that if I’d asked Mrs Pukeroa she would have told me it was a terrible idea and that the Cape was no place to go scattering ashes. It's tapu – sacred! Maybe that's why things went the way they did. Anyway, I didn't ask. I thought it was all simple. But *nomen omen*, says Mrs Pukeroa, which is Latin for 'with a name like Folly you're asking for trouble'. It wasn't simple. Not a bit.

Over the next couple of days I collected the things I thought I would need and hid them under my bed. All the riding gear was already in the paddock shed. The camping stuff was on a high shelf in the garage. I'd just climbed the stepladder and pulled out the pop-up when a voice almost sent me tumbling.

'What are you doing?'

Dylan was standing in the doorway.

'You nearly made me fall!' I tried to slide the pop-up out of sight.

Too late.

'What's that for?'

'Nothing. None of your business.' I climbed down.

'You're not allowed to touch stuff in the garage. I'm telling Dad.'

'No you're not.'

'I am too!' He started to back away.

No way was I going to let my pesky brother spoil everything. I dropped the tent and went for him.

'Oww!' He cried out as I squeezed his arm hard. I snatched Chewie away and held him up out of reach.

'Give him back!' Dylan started pummelling me with his fists.

'No. You're a dirty snitch and I'm going to snap his arms off.' I got ready to do it.

'Don't!' he squeaked. 'I won't tell!'

I gave him an evil stare. 'Promise.'

'I promise.'

'If you say anything to Dad or Audrey or anyone,' I hissed, 'I'll *end* Chewie in the wood chipper.'

Dylan's eyes widened in horror. 'Please give him to me,' he whispered.

Very slowly, I did. 'Remember,' I said, 'zip it – or else!'

Clutching Chewie to his chest, he nodded.

'Now scram!'

Once I'd ticked off the stuff on my list I took it all to the paddock in small lots on my bike.

'Easy on the luggage,' Tooth warned, chomping on an apple I'd brought him.

'There's hardly anything!'

'Says the one not carrying it . . .' Before I could think of a smart comeback he swished his tail and wandered off.

I looked at the pile. It really wasn't a lot – I didn't want to attract attention. And even though I had proper saddlebags, they would have looked too unusual. Instead I'd fold my sleeping bag under the saddle cloth and stuff the rest of the gear into my school backpack. Tooth and I would look like any other horse and rider out for an ordinary ride.

Not that he was so thrilled when I announced the plan.

'Can't it wait?' he said. 'There's a patch of ryegrass by the trough that's almost ready.'

'So? It'll still be there when we get back.'

He got that look like when I don't know what he means about the smell of rain coming, or the aftertaste of bad hay. 'You wouldn't understand.'

I had to promise to buy oats along the way.

'And peppermints. Lots.'

When I went down to breakfast on Thursday morning there was a small box by my plate.

I picked it up. 'What . . . ?'

Dad smiled, mysterious. 'Open it and find out.'

Inside were two white ceramic horses: a mare and foal.

I was collecting the set and Dad knew I'd been wanting this pair for a while.

'Not doubles, are they?' he said with a twinkle in his eye.

I shook my head. The lump in my throat was making it hard to say how beautiful I thought they were.

'Thanks, Dad,' was all I managed. Right then I felt terrible about deceiving him. I'd been wrong, he *did* understand. I wanted to throw my arms around him and tell him all about my crazy mission with Tooth. We could laugh over it together.

But he was already checking his watch. 'Oops, getting late. Dylan, in the car!' He ruffled my hair and gulped down the last of his coffee. 'Don't forget, slippery slide tomorrow.'

'Yay! Slippery slide, slippery slide,' chanted Dylan.

Something inside me went cold. I looked at the horses. They weren't a gift, they were a bribe. Dad was using them to buy my good behaviour for the outing with Audrey.

'I-I'm going to the library after school today,' I said as evenly as I could.

He was too busy hunting for his car keys to notice how angry I was. 'OK, I'll text Aud to let her know. Don't be back late.'

*Aud*. That did it – I became even more set on going ahead with my plan. Quickly I snuck into the lounge and went over to the cabinet with Mum's ashes. The door squeaked when I started to open it; I froze to listen in case Dad had heard, but he was still rounding Dylan up. Carefully I took the cylinder out and placed it in the bottom of my backpack. *I'll look after you, Mum,* I promised.

Outside I put the pack on my back, threw my school jersey into my carrier basket and got on my bike. Dylan pulled a scream face at me as the car backed out of the driveway. A moment later I was alone. I rode slowly along our street and the next, heading towards the river.

# 6

I spent the first few kilometres of the ride boring Tooth with how great the countryside was, but after hours of fields and fences and power lines the thrill wore off. Cicadas sawed. Magpies picked at roadkill. The sun bore down. I just wanted to get somewhere.

When I got hungry I stopped to take out the jam sandwich I'd made the night before while Dad and Audrey had been watching a movie. Tooth snacked on a clump of buffalo grass growing by the side of the road. Proper grazing would have to wait.

We reached Mamaranui at around four o'clock. It was the furthest I'd ever been on my own. I thought there'd be shops or something, but that's where maps fool you – in real life it was just a wide spot in the road, an empty crossroad.

'If we turn back now no one will know we were gone,' Tooth hinted.

'Forget it.'

'So far this trip hasn't been all that interesting.'

'Get used to it,' I snapped. The last thing I needed was a mutiny. Then I softened. 'Here, have a mint.' I reached forward in the saddle and he turned his head to snuffle it off my palm.

There was a bit more action in Kaihū. The souvenir place had a couple of tour buses in the parking lot. I recognised the turn-off to Uncle Dan's by the little church with the witch-hat spire and the cemetery plot beside it.

'See that big stone?' I pointed to a black marble tombstone so tall and shiny it was easy to pick out from the road. 'My cousin Susie says if you look at it by the light of a full moon something terrible will happen to you.'

'Really.'

'She did, and her appendix burst.'

It wasn't so simple to impress Tooth.

'The same Susie who called me Tufty?'

I'd forgotten about that. His mane does stick up a bit in places and he's touchy about it. Horses don't like being poked fun of any more than people. When kids at school call me Scarecrewe, I hate it.

'They took her to hospital by ambulance,' I went on.

'The Susie who rides that puffed-up chestnut?'

He knew perfectly well it was. Darcy was a dressage horse. Susie had won prizes with him.

'You're just jealous.'

'Sure. The strut.'

I giggled. Darcy *did* strut. He reminded me of a lifeguard in a TV show, parading on the beach.

'But your cousin thinks a dead rabbit's paw brings her luck, so they're a good match,' he went on.

I gave up. Once Tooth's made his mind up about someone, no amount of talk can change it.

At last we reached the turn-off. The sun was getting low to the treeline and I hurried Tooth along, anxious to find a place to camp for the night. I suddenly felt nervous. Back in town the library would be closing; soon Dad would find out I was gone. For a moment I worried about making *him* worry, but then I reminded myself angrily that it served him right.

'What about through there?' said Tooth as we passed a gap in the trees. By the way he kept twitching his ears I could tell he was keen to get down to grazing.

'It says on the map there's a holiday park around here. Let's get past that first.'

The park had bungalows and a campground. Some people were busy pitching tents and there was plenty of laughter and shouting as the kids got the flysheets sorted and pegged the guy lines. It gave me a twinge in my stomach. I'd never slept out on my own before and now that it was time to make camp, I wasn't feeling so brave. The sun had slipped even further down and the spaces between the trees looked dark and full of secrets. Who knew what might be lurking?

Alongside the entrance to the holiday park was a dirt track with a small bridge over a stream.

'What about along there? We'll be close to water.'

'I thought you wanted to get away from people,' said Tooth, but he must have picked up on my mood, because he didn't rub it in.

Just past the bridge we saw what looked like a side track with a clearing at the end. Tooth decided for both of us.

'This will be fine.' Without waiting to hear what I thought he turned down the track. In the clearing he put his head down and started tearing greedy mouthfuls of grass.

I dismounted stiffly. I wasn't used to such long stretches in the saddle. My sore arm ached. My legs ached. My bum ached.

'At last,' Tooth said when I unsaddled him and pulled off the sleeping bag pad. 'That thing was melting my kidneys.'

It was damp with sweat, so I laid it out on the grass to dry. I slipped off his bridle, then got out the small bag of oats I had brought and poured a few handfuls into a neat pile on the grass.

Tooth nickered with pleasure.

'Not stolen. Best I can do,' I said, stroking his neck. 'Thanks a million for being here.'

He nuzzled my arm and started chomping happily. While he ate I pulled the pop-up out of the bag. It opened out all wonky after being squashed up, but I got it right enough and dragged it to a leafy corner out of sight, along with the saddle and bridle. It was small and I'd have to lie curled up, but I didn't mind. For now it was home. Once I'd put my things inside it looked snug, like a nest. I set the cylinder with Mum's ashes by my pillow of clothes, hung Tooth's bridle on a branch and covered the saddle with my windbreaker against the dew.

That was camp sorted – now dinner. I lined the cans up on the grass. 'Pick a number from one to five,' I called to Tooth.

'Two.'

Cream-style corn. When I'd taken the cans from the cupboard at home I'd tried to find things I could eat cold without throwing up. The first spoonfuls tasted great – I was so hungry I could have eaten dog pellets – but by the end I was wishing he'd said four. That would have been peaches.

Things look brighter on a full stomach, Mum used to say – or maybe the corn just squashed out the loneliness. When I spread the map out and measured the distance we'd covered I felt a twinge of pride. We might not have come far yet, but here we were, trekking across the country all on our own!

Shadow fingers were reaching across the grass. I wanted to be settled for the night while it was still light – it would be risky to use a torch so close to the holiday park.

'Just going to get water.' I grabbed my drink bottle, along with the folding camp bucket I'd brought for Tooth, and headed for the stream.

The bank was lined with gorse and cutty grass, which screened me from the campsite on the other bank but was no fun to get past. I finally found a way through and half-scrambled, half-slid down to the water.

'Shh!'

I jerked back in surprise. It was a boy about my age. He was peering into a water hole, so caught up in what he was doing that he hadn't even bothered to glance my way. I could easily have crept off again and looked for another spot to fill the containers. But I was curious. Sidling over, I craned my neck to see.

He was dangling a hot dog on a string. Bait, but without a hook.

'Wait,' he whispered.

A moment later I couldn't help but gasp as the most

whopping eel I'd ever seen slid out from under some rocks. It was longer than a broomstick and thicker than my leg. As the boy jigged the string it swam in slow figure of eights. Finally it made up its mind and snatched one bite, then another.

The boy tied on another hot dog. 'Here, you hold it.' Very slowly, he passed me the string. Once I had it he reached into his pocket for his mobile and began taking photos. 'Bit higher,' he murmured. When I raised the bait the eel's glossy brown head broke the surface to follow it. Long thick lips, a beady eye . . . I nearly dropped the string.

'Ka pai – keep it there a sec,' said the boy.

The light was fading fast.

'She won't like this.' He snapped one last picture with the flash. Startled, the eel flicked away back under the rocks.

The boy laughed. He sat down on the bank and started going through the pictures. 'Your face when she stuck her head up! Look.'

He reached over to show me. It wasn't great that he had a

picture of me, but if I made a fuss and started asking him to wipe it he'd wonder why, so I left it.

'And this one: best shot yet,' he went on. 'It's because you were holding the string. When I do it, I can't get the angle.'

'Nice,' I said, though to be honest that mean-looking eye kind of put me off.

'I call her Nui.'

I'd never met a boy who photographed eels. I sneaked another sideways look at him. He seemed ordinary: dark hair, dark eyes, softish features. Nothing especially geeky.

'How do you know it's a she?'

'The biggest ōrea – I mean longfins – usually are.'

'It was humongous!'

'They can grow even bigger.' He turned, suddenly fierce. 'Promise you won't tell anyone about her!'

There was only Tooth *to* tell, but he didn't know that. 'I promise.'

'When it's her time she'll swim to Tonga, lay millions of eggs and die.'

'Bet she can't wait.' No wonder Nui was bingeing on hot dogs.

'But the babies come back!' the boy said quickly. 'Then the whole cycle starts again.'

'Ben!' a woman called over the water, adding something in Māori I didn't catch.

'Coming!' he yelled back. Then, to me: 'Dinner. Gotta go.'

'Are you with them?' I asked, pointing to the tents.

He nodded. 'We come every year.'

I felt a shot of envy. Not that I was overly crazy about camping – to my mind, for every good part like toasting marshmallows over the fire or telling creepy stories, there was always too much setting up to do and tents that leaked and imaginary axe murderers when you sprinted to the toilets after dark. But we'd been through it together, as a family. Now all the gear was just lying in the garage. Audrey wasn't the outdoorsy type.

'D'you like it?'

He shrugged. 'It's OK. I get some good pictures for my blog.'

'You blog *eels*?'

His eyebrows knitted together. 'So?'

'Nothing. I've just never met anyone who does, that's all.'

'It's not only eels . . . a while ago I posted a pretty good shot of a copper skink and a magazine used it for their cover.'

'Wow, nice.'

'Where's your family camped?'

I tensed. 'Uh, back there . . .' Waving vaguely behind me, I added, '. . . but don't tell. We're not really supposed to be there.'

Ben grinned. 'You keep my secret, I'll keep yours.'

It was almost dark. Tooth would be getting thirsty. I picked up the containers. 'I'd better get these filled.'

'Be-en!' This time the voice of the person calling was much younger. 'Mum says if you don't come now, you're on dishes!'

'Oops, better move it.' He started climbing the bank. Halfway, he turned. 'Are you allowed out after dinner? The campground owner told me there's a place with glow worms just up the road.'

I thought quickly. Ben seemed OK, and it wasn't as if I had better plans of my own – I'd probably just be lying alone in the pop-up trying not to think about axe murderers. Besides, I realised with a thrill, I could go where I wanted.

'Sure, I'll come.'

He looked pleased. 'Meet you half eight on the bridge, then. See ya!'

'Bye.'

He clambered up the bank and disappeared.

# 7

Tooth was still grazing. I mentioned the meeting with Ben and told him about Nui.

He shuddered. 'Brrr, ever had an eel slither under your belly in a full storm ditch? I have.' He drank gratefully from the bucket, plunging his muzzle deep and snorting droplets that sprayed my T-shirt.

It had been a long day for us both. Darkness settled, and only his munching disturbed the quiet. He'd still be eating when I got back from the glow worms. Horses need to graze a lot to keep up their energy.

I spread my sleeping bag out in the pop-up. It smelled of Tooth's sweat, but I didn't mind. Lying there with the tent flap open, watching his silhouette move slowly across the grass, I felt safe knowing he was there.

A ruru hooted, ready for the hunt. I yawned and groped in the side pocket of the backpack for my phone, sure there'd be loads of missed calls.

It wasn't there. I searched the other side and then everywhere else too, trying to ignore the flurry of panic in my chest. I knew I'd had it leaving home – I remembered switching it off going out the door and slipping it into the pocket. After that I hadn't used it. There'd been no need; I knew the way to Kaihū and the turn-off after that was signposted.

The truck. Had the phone slid out when I'd gone flying off my bike? It was the only explanation.

No phone. No way to call home. Not that I wanted to – the way I saw it Dad was meant to be calling *me*. I'd imagined him magically realising how hurtful the whole Auckland idea had been – enough to make me run away – and a whole stream of texts saying please come home. I suppose in my mind I'd been thinking that if he sounded sorry *enough* I might even forgive him and go back.

For a minute I thought the trip was over. Then I remembered Mum. If Tooth and I didn't finish what we'd set out to do, her spirit would stay troubled.

We'd show Dad what real caring looked like. I picked up the cylinder with Mum's ashes and hugged it to me in the dark.

'It's OK, Mum,' I said out loud. 'I don't need any stupid phone.'

Which was funny because that was what she used to tell me when she was taking it off me.

The paper map would have to be enough, and I still had a torch. If I really did need to get in touch with anyone, there were always internet cafés. The only problem now was knowing when to meet Ben on the bridge. I pinched myself to stay awake, but the yawns kept coming. I'd worried about being too scared to get to sleep – now I couldn't stay awake.

'Call me in a bit,' I told Tooth. At least I think I did. A minute later I'd fallen headlong into a dream.

His whinny snapped me out of it. Someone was coming! Torchlight swept the grass. The beam lingered on Tooth for a moment, then picked out the pop-up and blazed straight into my face.

'Stop it!' I scrambled to my feet, shielding my eyes.

The beam dropped and Ben came forward. 'It's me – I didn't mean to blind you.' He glanced back at Tooth. 'Is that your horse?'

I nodded.

'You're here all by yourself?' He sounded admiring.

There was no point denying it. 'Sorry I didn't make it to the bridge,' I said instead, to prevent more questions. 'When I got back here I just kind of crashed . . .'

''S OK. Still want to come? You don't have to.' He was

trying to sound offhand, but I could tell it was important. He didn't seem to care why I was camping on my own – the glow worms were what interested him. I relaxed.

'Yes!'

His smile looked even wider in the torchlight. 'Let's go, then – I have to be back in an hour.' As we started walking he asked, 'Hey, what's your name anyway?'

I liked him, so I only lied a bit.

'Holly.'

'I'm Ben.'

'I know, they called you for dinner, remember?'

'Oh. Right.' He stopped. 'Wait.' He dug a mini chocolate bar out of his pocket and snapped off half for me. 'I got it at the camp shop.'

'Thanks!'

We set off. Tooth lifted his head, but I gestured to let him know everything was OK and he went back to his grazing.

'I like your pony,' said Ben. 'He looks clever.'

Tooth pretended he hadn't heard, but I saw him cock an ear for more.

'He's good at gates,' I said, not wanting to give him a big head.

A short way down the road, a narrow track led into the bush. We barely spoke as we walked, but in the blackness even our footsteps sounded too loud. There was no moon. The torch slashed light across the trees and picked out red possum eyes. Small things rustled in the underbrush. I imagined all the creatures we couldn't see or hear and a shiver ran down my spine.

The first glow worms were dotted like fairy lights on the sides of the track.

'They're so pretty.'

'They're actually larvae. Like maggots,' Ben said helpfully. 'The glow is to attract insects. The hungrier they are the brighter it gets.'

'Well, for maggots they're really pretty.'

'The camp guy said something about a little cave. Told me to watch out for a pair of crossed trees.' We hadn't gone much further before he shone the beam on two trunks. 'Look, there!'

I'm not big on caves. The entrance to this one looked damp and sort of creeped me out. Then again, I definitely wasn't waiting outside on my own.

'He said it widens past the opening.' Ben turned off his phone torch and began groping his way forward.

I followed. I was just remembering all the things I hated about caving and wishing we could use the torch, when the first part opened up and we came out into a space about the size of a high-roofed car shed.

My jaw dropped. The ceiling was lit up like Christmas. *These guys must be starving*, I thought. But not even Ben's maggot facts could spoil the beauty. While he fumbled about getting ready to take a picture – without flash because light or noise would make the worms dim their glow – I gazed up open mouthed.

Till something dropped. Onto my tongue.

My scream was like a light switch: the whole cave went black.

'What? What's wrong?'

I was too busy gagging to answer, too terrified of swallowing. At last whatever was on my tongue flew out, just as Ben finally did the smart thing and turned on the torch.

'There . . .' I gasped, pointing at the ground.

When he shone the light I wished he hadn't. Pinned under the beam was a cockroach caged in sticky thread.

'That's a mucus trap. The roach was probably too heavy, so when it struggled . . .'

'IT WAS IN MY MOUTH!'

'Oh.' Ben shut up. Then: 'Ick.'

I raced for the exit. Outside I spat again to make sure the

sticky stuff was gone and took big gulping breaths, as if the night air could rinse my mouth clean.

'That was the grossest thing *ever*!' I told Ben when he joined me.

'You were like a cat puking fur balls.' He mimicked my slobbering, choking noises in the cave.

It sounded pretty funny. I giggled. A moment later the pair of us were bent over belly-laughing.

'Sorry you couldn't . . . get your photo,' I managed to say.

'I did!' He turned his phone screen to show me and I felt ill all over again.

'I can get a shot of the lights another day,' he said. 'It'll take a while for them to—'

I jumped as he suddenly gripped my arm.

'Hear that?' he hissed.

'Hear what?'

Ben put a finger to his lips and killed the torch. I froze, listening. The darkness thickened. I was just about to suggest we get out of there when some thin squeals rang out, like the cry of a mutant bat getting ready to swoop down and eat our livers.

'Kiwi!' Ben whispered. 'Now the female answers.' We waited. But the call that came next wasn't what he'd been expecting. 'Nah, just a weka.' Disappointed, he turned the torch back on. 'Come on, let's go.'

The walk back was less scary. I figured nothing could be worse than nearly swallowing a live roach.

'Thanks for coming with me,' Ben said when we reached the clearing.

'It was revolting. But kind of fun, too.'

Ben nodded. 'Are you still leaving tomorrow?'

'Uh-huh. I have to get to a place. Can you, um, not tell anyone?'

He nodded again, then shrugged. 'OK, well . . . bye, I suppose.'

'Bye. Give Nui an extra hot dog from me.'

'I will.'

We both hung about a moment longer, not knowing what else to say. Then Ben turned and started walking back to the campground. Just before the torch beam disappeared around the bend I heard him call out, 'I'll put you in my blog for the roach!'

I laughed. When he joined in, the sounds met in the darkness.

# 8

I woke with a crick in my neck. It was still dark, but birds were chattering. Nearly dawn. I opened the flap and stepped out. Tooth had been lying down not far away; hearing the zip, he scrambled onto all fours.

'Early start,' I told him, stretch-yawning.

He shook himself awake. 'One step ahead of the law?'

'We were probably all over the news last night.' I found the curry comb and gave his coat a quick brush.

'Hope the pictures showed my good side.'

'What good side?'

He paid me back with a soft nip.

As quickly as I could I packed everything away. My arm was stiff and sore to begin with, but it got better. *Day two,*

I realised – a whole night away on my own! They'd be looking for us now for sure. *Let them*, I thought, feeling pretty tough as I put the cylinder in and zipped up the backpack. We'd passed the first test. Now we needed to get into the forest.

Tooth was snatching bites of grass. I considered having breakfast before we hit the road, but decided it could wait. After tacking up I slung the pack on and hauled myself into the saddle.

The air was alive and fresh. The *clop-clop* of Tooth's hooves rang loud on the asphalt, but nothing moved as we passed the campground except a mother quail shooing her babies across the road. *Hurry, don't let them catch you!* she seemed to say. I thought of Ben and wondered how he'd be spending the day.

At the signpost I remembered something and got off again to rummage in the pack.

'What do you think?' When I tossed my head, the curls of Mum's real wig, the dark one, swished my cheek like a caress.

Tooth took one look and snorted. 'What good's that if they can still recognise the horse?'

'Don't worry, I've got something for you too.'

'Like what?' he said, suspicious, as if he was picturing himself with a fake palomino forelock.

I looked up mysteriously from under my brown fringe.

'You'll see.'

As the sun rose the lights of the milking sheds switched off and the indigo sky paled. The tarseal ended. A farm pick-up sped past, choking us in dust, but for the rest the road was ours.

I was chirpy as we jogged along. 'It feels like *ages* since we left. Can you believe this time yesterday I was in the kitchen at home having breakfast?' I pushed away the image of Dylan sitting opposite an empty place.

Tooth isn't really a morning horse. 'That ryegrass will be just right in a day,' he griped.

We reached the crossing and turned into Old Mill Road, hurrying past the cluster of houses before anyone spotted us.

The road took us to the edge of the forest. From there we could cut straight along an old coach track through the bush. The map said twenty-three kilometres. There were warning marks, but the other route was four times longer, so for me it was a no-brainer. Still, I checked with Tooth. It was only fair – we were in this together.

'What do you think?'

'I say the quicker the better.' He glanced at the belt of trees ahead and began snatching mouthfuls of grass as if they were his last.

The track sloped upwards at first, but the way was clear. It must have rained, because there was a lot of new growth. I saw emerald moss, a Cinderella-blue mushroom and baby fiddleheads. Bushes of ragwort, too.

'Keep away from that stuff, it's deadly. Uncle Dan's always hacking it out on the farm.'

'Yes, Professor.' Tooth makes fun of me when I tell him things like that. He says horses have been walking through their food long enough to know what it's supposed to look like.

We came to a place where supplejack vines hung over the track. I had my work cut out to keep them from snagging on the pop-up. I was still struggling to get one untangled as we rounded a bend, so when Tooth suddenly baulked and backed up without warning I lost my balance. One minute I was yelping with surprise, the next I was dangling over a slip.

The rains had torn away a whole chunk of the track. Only my grip on the vine was keeping me from a two-storey drop and a tumble down into the gully. My heart hammered. Every tiny movement set me jigging like a yo-yo, and the backpack was making it worse. Supplejack was strong, but any one of the branches supporting the vine could give way. My fingers were clamped so hard they ached. I couldn't see Tooth, but I heard his shrill whinnies. 'Stay back!' I cried. His weight might make more ground crumble.

The backpack was like a boulder pulling me down. But sliding each strap off to remove it would mean hanging by a single arm. Twice. I'd never have the strength. My bruised arm was already throbbing. I had to act fast. *Hold on, hold on, hold on* . . . The command was running on replay from my brain.

My feet were near the side of the slip. Moving slowly, not glancing down, I stretched one foot out and carefully dug a toehold with the tip of my boot. And another. Then I inched higher, making new steps and sliding my hands up the vine. Would it hold?

A clod of earth broke off. I couldn't stop myself from watching it drop. *If I fall* . . . I shut my eyes tight to block out the thought.

Hand over hand, toe after toe . . . When I drew level with the path I saw Tooth standing a few paces back, still spooked by his own near miss. Seeing me, he gave a worried nicker.

There was nothing he could do. I managed a couple more toeholds, then stopped. My arms were trembling. If I waited any longer my grip would fail. I could fall trying or fall not trying.

Biting my lip, I counted down for courage. *Three, two . . .* On one I pushed away from the slip face, using the vine like a rope swing, begging for it to hold. My body swung out and then back, feet straining for the highest toeholds. The vine held, but the weight of the backpack made me twist slightly in mid-air. One foot missed the mark. I planted the other toe, and with a shout of strain and fear I threw all my weight forward.

'Now!'

My fingers let go.

Good solid earth: for a long moment I lay still, letting my heart pound against it.

Tooth stretched out his neck and breathed into my hair. 'Sorry about that,' he said. 'Skittish of me.'

'No, you did right,' I mumbled into the dirt. The thought of him pitching headlong over the edge was too awful for words. We'd been lucky.

I wriggled forward to be sure I was in the clear, then slid the pack off and sat up to stare at the sliver of remaining track.

'No go,' said Tooth. Maybe he hoped I'd give up then and that we could just turn back and head for home.

'We'll find a way round,' I said instead.

When I stood up my legs were jelly. I had to grab the saddle for support. He stood like a rock, waiting for me to get my balance.

I lumped the backpack across the saddle and tied it in place.

We could hear running water – perhaps there was a way across somewhere below. Treacherous vines snaked over the slope. As we made our way down I took extra care placing my feet and warned Tooth to do the same. I couldn't carry him if he sprained a fetlock.

Finally we reached a creek. Tooth drank while I washed the mud off my face. I filled the water bottles before we headed back up to the track on the other side.

It wasn't much better on the path. For every stretch of flagstones from the old cart trail there were five lengths of mud to slog though. Tooth's hooves made squelching, farty sounds. Gloop trickled into my boots. Bits of track had been laid over with logs, but they'd rotted and could easily trap a hoof.

'Old Bog Road, more like it,' I grouched after losing a boot for the second time.

'At least it isn't winter.'

He had a point. I hadn't really thought about the weather when we'd planned the trip. It was summer – what could go wrong? This sort of ground wasn't what I'd been expecting.

It began to drizzle. Where the track narrowed it meant pushing through dripping plants, which didn't exactly cheer Tooth up.

'Wonder how my paddock's doing,' he mumbled, loud enough for me to hear.

'Oh, give it up.' My arm was hurting again. I was in no mood for grass gripes.

'I have. You made me.'

The rain made us both cranky. At last the track got firmer, but I still walked beside Tooth. Getting in and out of the saddle wasn't worth the effort and besides, I didn't want to give him more excuses to bellyache.

Around midday we came to a board map showing the route to Waimā.

'Waoku Coach Road, nine hours. Look, there's a Honeymoon Cottage – must be romantic.'

'Nine hours. Romantic.'

He was being a pain on purpose, but just then the sun came out and everything looked better. Raindrops twinkled khaki and emerald on the leaves and patches of clear sky showed through the high ferns. A tūī sang its whistle-click song.

'I'm starving, let's eat,' I said. There was no grazing, so I pulled out a carrot and an apple and the rest of the oats from the backpack for Tooth. Then I sat down on a trunk and had the peanut butter sandwich I'd been saving. It was a bit squashed, but the taste was just fine.

Tooth looked happier with something going into his stomach.

'You think there are people at this cottage place?' I asked between bites. 'Maybe we can sleep there.'

He didn't answer. I could see him thinking *People? Here?*

# 9

Not long afterwards we passed through a big stand of trees. The track was good and I had climbed back into the saddle. Rays of light filtered through the leaves and a mulchy smell rose from the ground. Birds flitted about on bird business. The forest felt deep and alive with activity. I was humming. Everything was going great. We'd reach the cottage in no time.

Then we hit another muddy stretch.

'It's better over there,' I said, pointing.

Tooth eyed the rooted-up ground. 'This is pig country. We should keep to the track.'

'Follow me.' I dismounted to lead the way.

An hour later we were both tired and footsore. Whenever

I tried to cut back towards the path something always seemed to bar the way. Tooth's mane and tail were clumped with burrs. His eye was weeping where a branch had struck it. My arms were scratched from pushing through prickly undergrowth. Mum's wig was matted with spider webs. It had been dumb to wear it where no one could even see us, but I'd just liked having it on.

I didn't want to admit we were lost. Under the canopy it got dark early and soon we wouldn't be able to go on. No one knew we were here. No one would come looking for us. My genius plan had been a huge mistake. Worst of all, Tooth wasn't saying anything. Whenever I stopped to try and get my bearings he just stood there slack-lipped, half-blinking his hurt eye.

It was drizzling again. The trees didn't seem wonderful any more, they were just trees. The bird twitter sounded mocking. 'Shut up!' I yelled. I was tired, hungry, cold. I'd been carrying the backpack – tied to the saddle, it caught on low branches – and at last I slung it down in defeat, biting my lip not to cry.

'What shall we do?' My voice sounded like the squit of an insect.

But instead of answering Tooth suddenly tensed and pricked his ears. Something rustled not far off. Was he thinking what I was thinking? Wild pigs, he'd said earlier. I'd heard too many of Uncle Dan's hunting tales about black razorbacks and dogs with their bellies ripped open not to shudder.

Whatever was making the sound was still hidden from sight, but we could hear it – the beast – drawing closer. I took firm hold of the reins. Tooth was charged and alert. The whites of his eyes flashed in the gloom.

A twig snapped. It was here! The reins tore from my hand as Tooth squealed in terror and pulled back, bolting through the trees. With a yell I plunged after him, fending off branches with my arms and stumbling over the lumpy ground.

'Wait! Wait for me!' I lost sight of him and blundered on in the direction I thought he'd gone. Behind me the beast kept coming. The faster I tried to go the more the branches fought against me. Twigs clawed at my clothes, leaves slapped me back. My breathing sounded jagged. I didn't know which way to turn.

I didn't see the root poking up. Suddenly I was sprawled on the ground, the reek of rotting leaves in my nostrils. Somewhere close, more twigs snapped: the beast had found me. I squeezed my eyes shut, waiting for the end.

'You got scalped.'

The beast talked? I rolled over, amazed.

She was holding up Mum's wig; it must have caught on a branch and I'd been too terrified to notice. She had on baggy old jeans, a checked bush shirt and an oilskin hat that shaded her face, but even in the shadows I could see the swirling lines of a moko on her chin. A hunting rifle was slung over her shoulder. A pair of dead possums hung round her neck on a string.

'This yours too?' My backpack was hooked over her shoulder with the rifle.

'Y-yes.'

She thrust out a hand. I shrank back, then realised she was only helping me up.

'What's your name?'

'Uh . . . Polly. From Waimā,' I said, then silently cursed myself. First rule of lies: never tell more than you have to.

The woman tilted her head to consider.

'You've come a fair way, Polly-from-Waimā.'

'We were going to my Uncle Dan's place in Kaihū but we got lost,' I blabbered. Now that I'd started, I might as well lay it on.

'We who?'

'Me and Tooth.' I looked around. If he was still charging off through the forest I'd never catch up with him. 'Did you see where he went?'

'The pony? Dead loss. Flighty. Trade him in, get yourself a good pig horse.' She spat onto the ground as if that settled it.

Out of loyalty I said nothing, but part of me agreed. Tooth had ditched me!

'I have to find him.'

'No worries, he won't get far.' She spat again. 'Well, I got fur to pluck. If you need a bed – which by the looks you do – you can stay at my hut and get going in the morning. Wouldn't want your uncle to worry.' She plopped the wig onto my head and strode off.

'But—' She was walking away with my backpack – and Mum's ashes! Part of my brain said to follow her. Maybe she could help me get out of the forest. But I couldn't just leave Tooth. He might snag a hoof or run into a real razorback.

'He went this way,' the woman called over her shoulder.

She was right. Soon afterwards we came to a clearing where a patched-together little cabin sat planted in the middle of the forest as if it had dropped out of the sky. It was a real hotchpotch. The boards were all different colours, the windows didn't match and the door had broken wooden frill around the edges and a cracked mirror in place of a window, like something that had once been part of a wardrobe. A concrete dog with one leg missing and a snapped-off ear kept guard on the porch. Helping it scare off unwanted visitors were four stripped tree trunks decorated with gruesome saw-toothed monsters made from scrap metal. Like totem poles. Or really tall nightmares. Moving in between them, the reins of the bridle dragging through the long grass while he stuffed his face, was Tooth.

The woman set my backpack down and headed for a lean-to shed on the side of the cabin with her catch. I marched straight over to Tooth. He barely glanced up. After the relief at knowing he was all right, the sight of him pigging out as if I didn't exist was too much.

'Thanks for chickening out on me, *friend*.' I slipped the bridle off and wiped the reins clean on my jeans.

He didn't bat an eyelid. 'I'm a horse. My brain says run, I run.'

'You didn't even care enough to come back!'

'Not true. I was just about to.'

'Sure, *after* dinner. I could be lying under a tree with my guts spilled.'

He went right on grazing. 'No sense letting the pig maul both of us. Also, I was starving.'

'There *was* no pig! It was *her*!' I tossed my head in the direction of the shed.

'So where's the problem?'

He was infuriating. I yanked the girth straps out of their buckles and pulled off the saddle and blanket.

'You know what? That woman's right. I should find another horse – one I can *trust*!'

Tooth wasn't having it.

'Well since we're talking trust, who was it that led us off track? "It's better over there, follow me" – wasn't that the line?' He gave a scornful snort and tore up another mouthful of grass.

We would have kept bickering all night if the woman hadn't poked her head out just then and called, 'How about you get the potbelly going?'

Tooth snickered. I shot him a black look, snatched up the gear and lugged everything to the porch of the hut, muttering that he deserved to get the runs.

# 10

The first thing I thought when I opened the hut door was that if I ever left *my* room that messy, Dad would flip. There were dirty clothes on the bed, dirty dishes on the table and old magazines and books piled up underneath it. Bundled pelts were stacked higgledy-piggledy against a wall. On a bench under the window lay a blow torch and a half-finished metal creation like something Dylan could have dreamed up. The place had a ton of clutter. But dried herbs and cured meat hung from a beam, and a three-legged armchair propped on a concrete block and draped in possum fur looked comfy by the stove.

The draught set a CD turning on a string in front of the window, flashing the last daylight across the walls. I found some matches and did my best with the stove, but by the time the woman came in there was soot all over me and still no flame. She hung the skinned animal she'd brought in on a hook, lit the storm lamp over the table and came to watch me burning my fingers. Shaking her head, she pulled out half the kindling I had packed in and showed me how to let the flames breathe.

'Beats me what they learn you kids at school.'

Her name was Kiri.

'"Cactus Kiri", the farmers call me,' she said as she diced onion for the stew, '. . . cos of them.' She tossed her head in the direction of the posts outside.

'I can sort of see how they might,' I said, trying to be polite.

She laughed. It came out more like a bark – you could tell she hadn't practised in a while. Now that her hat was off I could see her dark hair and the strong lines of her face better. She was younger than I'd thought. Younger than Dad. All except her eyes – they were old.

'Only hunters and greenies come this deep into the forest.'

She glanced at me. 'Once in a blue moon a pony girl. Anyway, not to brag or anything, but I think I'm what they call a local oddity.' She scraped the onion into the pot and added herbs and chunks of meat. 'Yesterday's catch,' she made sure to point out. 'Fresh possum tastes like a skunk's behind. The meat has to hang a day or two. I had a couple that were ripe.'

Hearing about it was making me feel sick. Maybe I could have one of my cans instead. But when I glanced across at her, Kiri's moko seemed twisting and alive in the shadowy light. I let the idea go.

'Pity we haven't got mushrooms,' she was saying, putting the pot on the stove to simmer. Secretly I was glad. I hate mushrooms.

The stew tasted better than it had sounded. After dinner Kiri padded an overturned crate for me and made some tea. The stove gave off a cosy glow.

'Here.' She held out a mug. There were scratchy little tats inked on her fingers, like the ones the older kids do in class when they're bored.

The tea was good and sweet, the way I like it.

'Is this Honeymoon Cottage?' I asked, suddenly wondering if Tooth and I had got our distances all wrong.

Kiri chuckled. 'Nope, you'd have passed that coming over from Waimā.'

I kicked myself inside. 'That's right. I forgot.' Quickly I switched to a different subject. 'Did you make this hut yourself?'

'Uh-huh.'

'Why?'

'I needed a place to lay low and think.' She hooked the stove door open with a stick and tossed in a log.

Was she on the run too? I didn't dare ask.

'It must have taken ages to build.'

'A while. Straightening nails was a job.' Seeing my puzzled face she added, 'I got everything from salvage.'

That explained the patched-together look.

She shut the stove again and we sat in silence, listening to the wood hiss. After a while I told her, 'I'm kind of laying low myself. There's this job I have to do.'

Kiri nodded as if she understood about important jobs. We were both quiet, until I pointed to the creation on the bench.

'Do you make those to scare people off?'

'Uh-uh. They're for the bad spirits.' She twirled a finger in the air as if there might be some hovering at that very moment.

Was she serious? She'd said it like the most normal thing in the world. Not knowing what to say myself, I stared at my feet.

She was still holding the stick and all at once she banged

it down hard between us, making me jump. 'This is the hut.' She pointed to the sooty mark the tip had left on the boards. 'And this . . .' – she traced a big area around it – '. . . is forest. How long before those tricksters start buzzing round again if I don't keep them back?' She snapped her fingers. '*This* long.'

Her deep-set eyes were drilling straight into mine. I was just thinking it would have been better to take my chances in the forest than spend the night cooped up with a possum lady who thought demons were on her case, when an idea suddenly came to me.

'Have you ever seen a ghost?'

She laughed and leaned back in the armchair, the tension broken. 'Nope. Some wairua, though. Souls, spirits.'

'Wow.' I was impressed. 'I've only seen one. My mum's. She died not so long ago.' My voice wavered a bit as I said it.

Kiri nodded and asked in an easy way, 'She visits often?'

I described how Mum's shimmer had been popping up and she listened as if I was telling her the sky was blue.

'What's she trying to tell me? What does she want?'

'Ask her. They like it when we talk to them,' Kiri said.

I wanted to know if my idea of going to Cape Rēinga was a good one, but before I could get a word in about where Tooth and I were headed, Kiri put a finger to her lips. 'Best keep that to yourself,' she warned, throwing furtive glances around the room as if the mean spirits might be listening. 'You don't want any bad energy spoiling your plans.'

She was trying to help. But the way things turned out, plenty of bad energy mucked our plans up even without me blabbing them out loud. If I had told her, I might have found out about the Cape being tapu and chosen somewhere else to go. That would have changed everything.

She told me how to get back to the track by following some tags she'd laid out in her early days in the forest.

'Once you're on the coach road you can think about which way you're going.'

'I—'

'That's your business,' she said, talking over me. 'I'd set you on course myself, but I sleep late and you'll be leaving early.' I got the feeling she was setting the deadline for me to be gone. 'You can bunk down there.' She gestured toward the bed in the corner. 'I'll be up most of the night anyway.'

I stifled a yawn. It had been a big day. Mumbling something about having to check on Tooth, I got up from the crate. I did it in such a rush that I lost my balance. Kiri gripped my arm to steady me.

'Ow!' Her fingers were pressing right into the bruise from the accident.

She let go. Then, gently, she slid my sleeve up.

'You fall off old Flighty?' she asked when she saw the bruise. I was going to tell her it was a bike I'd fallen off, but she was already on her feet, saying, 'I know something for that.'

With the stove stick she unhooked a bunch of leaves hanging from a beam to dry. Tearing off a handful, she put them in a pot and poured hot water on top. While they were soaking she found a strip of clean cloth. When the leaves were soft she made a pad of them and bound it over the bruise. At first it was so hot I could hardly stand it, but it cooled fast.

'Leave it on while you sleep,' Kiri told me. She went to the bench, adding over her shoulder, 'Tell that pony of yours he better not even think about scratching his itchy backside on my posts.'

That made me wonder if she'd heard Tooth and me talking, but she had already sat down to work and I didn't want to disturb her by asking. Pulling on a hoodie, I went outside. It was so dark I almost ran straight into Tooth.

'What's she like?' he asked. He'd calmed down. I was over our tiff too. That's another thing I like about us: we let stuff go.

'Bit strange, but OK. We had possum stew.'

'Blech.'

'It wasn't so bad.'

'Can she help us get out of here?'

'There's a trail. First thing in the morning we leave. I said we were going to Uncle Dan's.'

'Mmh.'

'To throw her off the scent,' I added quickly, before he got started about it being a terrific idea.

He sighed. 'Of course.'

'Maybe she didn't believe me, but it doesn't matter. I don't think she talks to other people much.' I passed on her message about the posts.

'Her prickle sticks are safe with me,' said Tooth.

'Brr.' I pulled up my hood. Even in summer it was chilly in the forest after dark. It would have been a cold night in the pop-up. 'You OK out here?' I asked.

'I'll manage.'

I slung an arm over his neck and leaned against him,

breathing in his scent. He smelled good the way only a horse can. The clearing made a cookie-cutter circle of night sky above us, with a swoosh of Milky Way through the centre. I read that it can take so long for the light of some stars to reach us that when their lives end we don't see them disappear until thousands of years later. If Mum had been a star I wouldn't have had to know for ages and ages that she'd died.

All the gazillion pinpoints suddenly reminded me of the glow worm cave. I snapped my mouth shut. But a minute later I wondered aloud to Tooth, 'Do horses read stars?'

'The bright bits? They're just holes.'

'No, before they collapse.' We'd learned about the Universe in class so I knew dead stars could become black holes. 'When they're still stars.'

'Holes, you mean.'

It was no use, Tooth sees the world differently. 'They're made of gas,' I said, wanting to have the last word.

'That's nice.'

We said goodnight. On the porch I pulled the pop-up out of the pack and rummaged for the cylinder of ashes to take inside so I could keep it close during the night. Kiri was at the bench, so caught up in her work that she didn't notice when I wished her goodnight too. I went to bed.

Next morning I was woken early by something hopping about on the roof. Kiri was sprawled asleep at the bench. It wasn't until I'd saddled Tooth and was about to pick up the backpack that I saw the keepsake she'd made for me out of tin during the night, resting on one of the straps. It was a bit bigger than a two-dollar piece, with a ragged spiky edge like a sun or a fireball. Scratched across it in letters as rough as the tats on her fingers was the word *kaha*: strong. I put it in my pocket and we set off to find the markers.

# 11

Waimā was just a word on paper, but Rawene had a courthouse and a Baptist church and a proper takeaway shop. Before we'd left the forest I'd painted four white socks onto Tooth's legs using a tube of tempera I'd brought along from my Young Picasso art box. I'd changed into fresh clothes and brushed the cobwebs out of Mum's wig, so coming into town the pair of us were looking pretty sharp. The bruise on my arm felt a whole lot better too. Whatever leaves Kiri had used, they'd worked.

In a tiny internet café I went online. Not that I was hanging out to connect with anyone and besides, it was better not to leave a trail, but Ben had told me the name of his website and I wanted to take a look. It was neat, a little technical maybe, but with great photos and even a couple of pretty decent jokes. He'd uploaded a picture of Nui and the one of my cockroach, too, just like he'd promised, with *Caught by Holly. Tau kē – cool!* written underneath. In the comments I wrote:

**Holly the roach poacher**

Kia ora, Ben, how's Nui doing? Has she eaten you out of pocket money yet? Is she ready for Tonga?

I picked up some breakfast oats at a dairy for Tooth and left him waiting outside the takeaway place. 'Ask if they have watermelon,' he said as I went in. They didn't, but I got him pineapple fritters instead and splashed out on cheese chips and deep-fried banana-ice-cream pie for myself.

The news was playing on a flatscreen in the corner. There was a story about a big drug ring and something about the government, and then the news guy was saying how divers were still searching for the body of a missing Dargaville schoolgirl presumed drowned in the Wairoa River.

The girl was me. They'd gotten hold of that terrible school photo where I still had braces and my hair was braided tight because someone in class had nits. I looked like Heidi. The reporter said that a school jersey with my name on it had been found hanging over the road barrier by a passing jogger. When she'd seen the bike, the jogger had contacted the police. The reporter went on to say it was anyone's guess how far my body had been carried by the current. My phone had been lying under a bush. There was a video clip of the bike with its twisted wheel, then shots of our house with police cars in the driveway and Dylan's toys on the lawn.

I went white-cold inside. 'Presumed drowned' . . . Before Dad had even had time to realise I was gone the police must have been calling him at work to tell him there'd been an accident and to get ready for the worst. I was still taking in the words when a close-up of his face came on. Someone had put ten extra years on him. As he talked to the reporter the camera moved onto Dylan and closed in on his little hand gripping Chewie.

Shame washed over me. What kind of person was I? People were looking for us all right, but not the way I'd imagined. A lump jammed in my throat. How could I put my family through something so terrible? I wanted to shout at the screen that I was alive so they could all hear me. I wanted to race into Dad's arms and beg him to forgive me.

The camera panned back. Dad was next to Dylan, holding him close. His other arm was around Audrey's waist. 'We just want to bring our girl home,' he was saying, while Audrey stood there nodding like a bobble head.

Something inside me snapped. We? Our? What did Audrey have to do with anything – she wasn't my mother! Why was she even in the picture?

'Number twenty-five,' called the woman at the till. I paid in a daze and took my order outside.

'What's wrong?' asked Tooth, seeing my expression.

'Nothing.'

'Did they have watermelon?'

'No!'

'Calm down, I was just asking.'

I looked around. The sun was blazing. Water twinkled in the harbour. A lawnmower droned and the smell of cut grass wafted across the road. Nothing was wrong except that everyone thought I was dead and I had lost my family forever. I wanted to howl.

When I finally told Tooth about the news story he said the game was up and that I should call home. I wouldn't do it. I hadn't drowned, but a part of me *felt* dead. I think until then I'd been counting on pretty much everything going my way. We would make it to the Cape. Mum's spirit would be at peace. Dad would be shocked into remorse and weepily thank me for teaching him the hard truths he'd been too duped to see. When she realised her hold on him had broken, Audrey would explode like a supernova and be composted into the galaxy. Auckland would fall off the map.

Instead I was the one being pushed out. I could never go back. I would live the rest of my life like this, moving from town to town and never settling down. Maybe one day I would get in touch with Dylan again, but for now the only thing that still made sense was finishing what I had set out to do.

There was more bad news at the ferry landing. Rawene was on one side of the harbour and we had to cross over to the other. There was no bridge. The car ferry ride only took fifteen minutes, but Tooth wasn't a car.

'Sorry, luv, no can do,' the ferry master said as we were about to go on board. 'Safety rules.'

My face fell. 'But how will we get across?'

'Have to take the long way – unless that pony of yours can

paddleboard.' He chuckled at his own joke, then gave me a wink. 'Better call the mum and dad taxi.'

'The long way' meant skirting round the whole harbour. It would add days to our trip and we didn't have the food or the money for that. I didn't even bother to ask Tooth what he thought. He'd probably jump at the chance to call it quits.

The ferry left without us. Near the landing was a public area with swings, and not knowing what else to do, we made our way over to the picnic table. As I set the food down and dumped the pack on the bench I did a double take.

'Where's the pop-up?'

We both stared. The tent didn't miraculously appear. Suddenly I remembered: Kiri's porch. In my mind I could see the long bundle lying where I had tossed it aside to take out the cylinder.

Great, now I didn't even have shelter. I slumped onto the bench and put my head in my arms. I felt like crying. I *did* cry. Everything was terrible.

# 12

It would be an hour before the next trip. Tooth nuzzled the takeaway wrapping open and picked out a fritter with his teeth. I pushed the package away. Maybe he could chow down as if nothing was wrong, but I'd just found out my life was wrecked forever. I'd choke if I ate.

A camper van arrived at the landing. The parking area for the next ferry was still empty, but the driver chose a space at the back of an imaginary queue, not far from where I was sitting, then got out and lit himself a smoke. He was weedy like a jockey, with greasy dark hair and pock-marked skin. Wraparound sunglasses hid his eyes. He looked to be wound up pretty tight, snatching quick, nervous drags on the cigarette as he slid the side door of the van open and got in to check something in the back. When he'd finished and was pulling the door shut again, his mobile rang.

'Yep. All set,' I heard him say.

Tooth had been chewing on the fritter, and right at that moment he choked on a piece of pineapple. He started coughing and wheezing to clear his throat. The man turned around to see what was going on, the phone still pressed to his ear, just as the chunk flew out and landed close to his feet. He stared down at the slimy lump and up at Tooth again. Then he turned on his heel and walked off towards the waterfront café.

'Forgot to lock up,' Tooth said when he'd recovered.

'So?' I was spoiling for a fight. Tooth moved away to graze, leaving me festering. I stared across the harbour. The dunes on the other side shone like gold just out of reach. 'It's not fair!' I ranted to myself. 'What's so dangerous about a *horse*? Those cars could be carrying *any*thing – what if one of them ex*ploded*?' At each angry word I stabbed my pocket knife blade into the wooden table. It made me wild to think such a stupid rule was going to kill our whole journey. '*Any*thing,' I said again, gouging the wood.

Then I stopped. An idea had just come to me that might work, but only if we were quick. The landing wouldn't stay deserted for long. Scooting over to the driver's cabin, I peeked inside – yes, there was a partition sealing it off from the back. The rear door was on our side of the van and pretty much completely out of view. I double checked the landing anyway for watchful eyes. All clear. Now what if we . . . ?

A few stealthy moves later, Tooth was sandwiched between a sink and a mini-fridge and I was perched on a bunk bed with my legs dangling over the side.

'This is crazy,' he muttered, shifting his feet.

'But *good* crazy if it gets us across,' I whispered back. 'Just stay still.'

He gave a nicker of protest. 'When that man opens the door he'll have a heart attack and then we'll get arrested.'

'We'll probably get arrested anyway, remember?'

The driver took his time coming back, which suited us fine – the less time he spent in the van, the less chance we had of being discovered. But the hour dragged. It was dark and stuffy cooped up inside. I didn't dare open the shades, but we could hear doors slamming as cars began to arrive and people got out to stretch their legs and look for somewhere cool to wait. Tooth dozed.

The bleep of the key startled us both. The van had been left open, so now the driver had locked it without realising. Would he notice his mistake and come to check the back? I held my breath as he tried the front door handle. But he only muttered something and bleeped the key again. After a moment the van's revving engine added to the chorus of motors starting up around us. I breathed again. The ferry had returned.

The driver couldn't see us. All we had to do was keep very still and very quiet. *Don't. Move*, I mouthed to Tooth when the van finally loaded.

He rolled his eyes: *No. Kidding.*

A horn sounded. As the ferry pulled away I felt a little skip of hope. Soon we'd be across the harbour. I pictured us already cantering away on the other side and me calling out to the ferry master: 'We paddleboarded!'

But to do that we'd have to get out of the van, and if we wanted to be ready to grab our chance I had to see outside. Carefully, I slid one of the shades open the tiniest fraction.

We were parked in the left rear corner, with only one other car, a white SUV with tinted windows, between us and the side. Beyond the railing the water sparkled like a scatter of diamonds. The van was baking hot in the sun; Tooth's coat was damp with sweat. The water looked so cool and inviting I wished I could join the cormorants diving for fish.

It took a moment before I noticed the driver's door of the

SUV opening and a hand reaching down through the bottom gap to empty an ashtray onto the deck. In a trice the breeze sent ash and cigarette butts skittering under the car into the sea.

The driver's seatbelt caught in the gap of the door when he tried to close it again. As he reached round to free the belt I got a glimpse of heavy-lidded eyes and a mouth set in a faint sneer.

I pulled back fast. Had he seen me? No, he couldn't have. But my heart was pattering double time. The eyes had been so hard, so cold. I shuddered.

Tooth nickered softly. 'What's wrong?'

'I . . . nothing.' I counted to ten and peeked out once more. The car door was shut, the smoked glass window screening the driver from view. I sank back against the wall.

Seconds later we both nearly jumped out of our skins as the back door of the camper van slid partly open. A hand reached in to dump first one, then another sports bag on the seat by the exit. The door banged shut. After a moment I heard what had to be the SUV door closing.

Tooth and I stared at each other. *What—?* But there was no time to figure it out – already the horn was sounding. We'd reached the other side.

If I thought that would be our chance to get out, I was wrong. The driver steered the van off the boat and kept right on going. A short way down the road the SUV overtook us and roared off.

Once we were really moving Tooth had some footwork to do to keep his balance. If it hadn't been for the carpet on the floor and the rugby on the radio, the driver would surely have heard him.

That wasn't the only problem. The road we were travelling on was all curves.

'Your face is a new colour,' Tooth said helpfully.

I slid a window open and closed my eyes, trying to stop feeling pukish. *Think about something else.* Practically on command the words 'presumed drowned' popped into my head. My thoughts began whirling faster and faster: police cars–Dylan's hand–smashed bike–Dad's face–fast river–Audrey's face–smashed bike–fast river–Dad's face–police cars . . . the images strobed over and over on repeat until I couldn't bear it any more and jerked my eyes back open.

I had no clue where we were going. All I knew for sure was that Tooth was getting more and more fidgety. Finally I guessed why.

'Don't you dare!' I hissed. But he did. A moment later there was a steaming pile on the carpet.

The stink was tremendous, like six farts in a sleeping bag. I had to peg my nose. If the front cab hadn't been sealed off the driver would have fainted at the wheel.

Tooth tossed his head. 'This ride was a bad idea. I want to get out.'

'We can't.'

'We can.' His nostrils crimped and the stubborn glint in his eye meant he was probably going to make it happen whether I liked it or not.

Just then the van slowed down. I'd slid the window shut, but through a tiny gap in the blind I could see we were coming into a small town. This was it: showdown. The driver must have caught a whiff after all – as he backed into a parking space and turned off the engine I shot Tooth a poison glance: *See? Your fault!* I racked my brains for a really good lie, but none came. The bottom line was we'd stowed away and Tooth had used the camper as a toilet. The driver would throw a cat fit. Our only hope was to be ready and move fast to make the most of the surprise factor. Once we were out we'd make a break for it. I hoped there were people about – he couldn't do anything bad to us in public, could he?

But the radio kept playing. The game was still on. It might be we weren't the reason he'd stopped after all.

'YEEEEESS!' we heard him shout. The crowd was going wild too, so his team must have been doing something good. Then the cheering was suddenly cut off and the door slammed. Tooth and I froze.

The sound of the remote lock snapped us out of it. I peeked out on the steering wheel side and saw the driver on the pedestrian crossing, heading towards a dairy on the other side of the road. Maybe he'd run out of smokes. Whatever – this was our chance.

'Come on!' I said to Tooth.

We were all ready to go and I was helping him reverse in the tight space, when he bumped against one of the sports bags on the seat. It fell onto the carpet with a soft thud, blocking the entrance way.

I swore. We didn't have time for hitches. The passage was so narrow I had to lean over behind his rump to grab the bag by one handle. I'd lifted it far enough to grab the other handle and was about to heave it back onto the seat when something stopped me.

Pulling on it had eased the zip of the bag partly open. Inside I could see what looked like tightly coiled rolls of paper held fast by rubber bands. I opened it wider and took one roll out. It was a fat bullet of banknotes. *Lots* of banknotes. I glanced down. The bag was full of money.

# 13

I still don't know why I did it. I suppose seeing the TV report had really shaken me. Until then, in my mind there had always been a 'Going Home' chapter at the end of the story. Now the pages were blank. Maybe the idea flashed through my head that if Tooth and I were going to live on our own for the rest of our lives we'd need money to get started. Before I'd even thought things through properly, I was crawling between Tooth's hind legs – dodging dung – to start chucking handfuls of the rolls into my backpack.

Tooth glanced back and saw what I was doing. 'Are you allowed to do that?'

'Sure!' I bluffed. He looked doubtful, but as he says himself, he doesn't always understand people rules about who owns what. For instance, the idea that one animal thinks it can call another animal 'mine' is deeply weird to him. He said nothing.

The zip snagged when I tried to close it. There was no time to fiddle with it. I left the bag on the seat, slung my pack on again and reached for the door handle. That's when I paused. Was helping myself to someone else's money really such a smart move?

It was too late to change my mind. I tugged the handle. My heart lurched when the door didn't move – *We're locked in!* – but it had the kind of safety lock you can open from inside and when I pulled harder it slid back. I jumped out and gave the all clear. Tooth backed down onto the footpath after me, one hoof at a time.

The best way to ruin everything would be to charge off like a pair of bank robbers. I eased the door shut, trying to look as if Tooth and I travelled by camper van every day of the week. But my heart was pounding.

There were plenty of people shopping. Christmas wasn't far off. Out of the corner of my eye I saw a little boy staring at us and tugging on his mother's arm – 'Mummy, look!' – but she was too busy sorting money for the parking meter. Two girls wearing identical rainbow-lens sunglasses giggled as they walked by. Other people hardly even glanced our way. Maybe they were used to this kind of thing. After all, it was farm country. Auntie Nora once took a calf to the sale yards in the back seat of her Ford Fiesta.

'Over there,' I murmured, nodding towards a side street. We needed to put distance between ourselves and the van. I led Tooth by the reins along the footpath. We passed a pharmacy with an air puppet Santa dancing by the door and a yappy terrier tried to bark us off the footpath, but he wasn't fazed. I had my fingers crossed, praying the van driver wouldn't come back. At the cinema on the corner we turned into the side street. I didn't climb into the saddle. It was better not to stick out. We just melted away, like heroes in a zombie movie trying not to trigger an apocalypse.

I found a supermarket and left Tooth hitched to a signpost in the parking lot while I topped up our supplies. Back outside I arranged everything properly in the backpack. My school uniform was only taking up space; I chucked the polo shirt into the nearest bin but kept the black shorts for spare. Then I checked the map again.

'See? Three more days, sand all the way.' I whooshed my finger up Ninety Mile Beach like a slide, even though we'd both learned by now that maps can play tricks.

Tooth looked about as excited as concrete.

'You'll love it,' I went on chirpily. 'No fences for as far as you can see.'

'Fences mean grass,' he said. 'Is there grass?'

I didn't know, but his back-pedalling was starting to wear

on me so I changed the subject to get him in a better mood. There was a sports shop on the other side of the road with a big rugby ball on the sign.

'Remember the time you wandered onto the rugby field during that game?'

It worked. He gave a whinny-snort and said with a little toss of his head, 'They loved me. I got a lot of applause, especially when the linesman tried to catch me.'

I laughed. One Saturday he had found the gate open – or opened it himself, he'd never let on which – and decided to go walkabout. Dargaville High were playing Rodney College at the rugby park and Rodney were running the home side ragged. Our neighbour's daughter was in the team and she told me afterwards that Tooth had trotted on just as Rodney's star fullback had been about to convert another try. The game stopped and Tooth did some of his slalom specials before he let himself be caught, which gave the Dargaville girls the breather they needed. Rodney still beat them, but by less, and Tooth was a bit of a hero for helping them save face.

It was nice to see him looking more cheerful, so I went on talking about it with him, letting him relive the glory.

'I ducked and dodged,' he said. 'Someone called out "Sign him up!"'

He'd told me before but it still made me laugh. Then I jumped as a jokey voice behind me said, 'A chatty one, is he?'

A smartly dressed businessman walked past us towards his car. Had he really overheard Tooth? Most people *don't* listen, what Tooth had said in our early days was true, but I still held back when others were around. The man had startled me, coming up on us like that. While he was fishing out his keys he winked at me like I was some little kid he'd caught talking to a teddy bear.

'Stupid muffinhead. What would he know,' I muttered as he drove off. I didn't like our friendship being made to look silly.

Tooth was still lost in the memory glow of his big crowd

moment. Now I was the one out of sorts. I force-steered my thoughts onto the problems at hand. The new ones. Before going into the supermarket I'd had a better look at the stolen money. It had turned out to be all hundreds. A kid my age with that kind of cash? Sure. In the supermarket I'd tried paying with one of the notes anyway, but the girl on checkout had rolled her eyes and said they only accepted real money, thank you.

Taking the cash had been a mistake. I'd left one of the bags jammed open and besides, I'd pinched too much for it not to be noticed. When the camper driver found out part of the stash was gone and saw the dung on the carpet, he'd remember the pony choking up pineapple on Rawene landing. He'd be after us at warp speed.

'Dung? Prime fertiliser!' said Tooth when I gave him another earful about it. 'Great for roses.'

'Gangsters don't grow roses.'

It was a cash drop, just like in a movie. Bank robbery loot or money being shuffled around on the sly for some kind of illegal deal. I was sure the ashtray guy had been the one to put the bags in the camper – after all, I'd heard the SUV door shut. I knew we were in big trouble, too – bigger even than the *other* trouble. I could throw the money into the nearest bin, pretend I'd never seen it. But there was a stinking trail that told the camper-van driver exactly who'd helped themselves to the cash. Whoever the money belonged to, they'd come looking for it. They'd still be after us.

I'd told Tooth about the SUV guy, but held back on the rest. If I spilled the whole mess he'd make a beeline for his paddock. I'd probably have swung a U-turn for home myself if something hadn't happened right then to stop me.

Mum.

Seeing her was so unexpected I caught my breath. Tooth's ears pricked immediately at the sound.

'Over there, look,' I murmured.

'I see dry grass, then a bad-tasting plant, then a signpost. Am I missing something?'

She was already gone. Maybe no one else *could* see her. It didn't matter. What mattered was that she knew we were on the road and she was travelling with us. It was all I needed to remember why we were doing this in the first place. We had to keep going.

Tooth was happy to stretch his legs after the tight space of the camper and I was happy to be leaving trouble behind, but it seemed to take ages to make any headway. It wasn't his fault. We were going at a steady clip, but the countryside was so flat it felt as if we were hardly moving. That had been one good thing about the van – we'd covered a bit of distance fast.

'When are we going to get somewhere?' This time it was me doing the grumbling.

Tooth didn't mind the scenery at all.

'I like a good clear view,' he said. 'Less to worry about.'

I jumped at the chance to show off.

'Maybe that's because a long time ago horses lived on the open plains and got used to being able to smell or see other animals hunting them.'

'Maybe.'

'Horses can gallop faster than fifty,' I said as we passed a road sign with the driving limit painted on it. 'You could get a ticket for speeding.'

'Fancy that.'

'And your ears can turn one-eighty degrees.'

'What do you know.'

I was jabbering horse stuff to stop from thinking about not-horse stuff. The stolen money was burning a hole in my peace of mind. There was a clenched feeling in my stomach. I needed someone to tell me what to do.

Mum never gave up fighting, but she knew she wasn't going to make it. About a month before the end she gave me a notebook.

'Just some bits and pieces I've been thinking about. Might come in handy later.'

She was trying to keep her voice light, but we both knew what was going on. I couldn't look at her; I just stared at the book. The cover was pale blue. She had written *For Folly* and drawn a little heart underneath.

Right then I decided I was never going to open it. The notebook was one of those magic tests to trick me, like in a fairytale. As long as I didn't look inside, I could keep Mum instead. That way she could tell me the bits and pieces herself.

Maybe she sensed what I was thinking.

'There's no hurry to read it. I'm here now.' She put her arms around me and held me close. I could feel the beating of her heart, the warmth of her body and the rise and fall of her breathing. We stood there for a long time, not saying anything.

The notebook wasn't magic. Not opening it didn't help.

After she died I was so mad I flung it into my dresser drawer without looking at a single page. It was still there.

Whatever Mum had written in it, I was pretty sure none of it was about running away from home and getting mixed up with gangsters and how to get rid of a load of money you'd taken and didn't want any more. If she'd known how to backtrack on stuff that bad she would have done it herself and gotten well again.

'Hey! You! What do you think you're doing?'

I snapped to attention. While I'd been caught up daydreaming, Tooth had taken a detour to snack on some tender leaves in a front garden with no fence. A crabby-looking old woman with her hair in curlers was scowling at us through an open sliding glass door.

'Get your horse off my lawn! If it's eaten my dog rose you'll hear about it!' She stepped out onto the deck and started coming towards us.

I didn't hang about waiting for her.

'S-sorry!' I called, turning Tooth away to get out of there at a speedy trot. I could hear the woman shouting after us as we cantered off along the verge.

'Did you have to?' I asked once we were far enough away to slow down again.

Tooth didn't bat an eye.

'We also like sweet plants,' he said, putting in a horsey fun fact of his own.

# 14

We reached Awanui and went straight to the only café, a place called Carol's Drop In that did food and internet. Carol was a big blonde woman in a lavalava and an XXL T-shirt with a glittery pink skull on the front. When I asked if Tooth could graze out the back she said, 'No problemo. Make my lazy son happy.'

'Yeah, save me some mowing,' grinned a young man with a quiff from behind the grill, not looking up from the patties he was flipping.

I left Tooth happily munching on the patch of overgrown lawn behind the building and went back inside to buy a can of lemonade.

'Matt, I'm popping out to get that tyre changed,' Carol was telling her son. 'Keep an eye on things, OK?'

I asked him for the lemonade and started digging in my pockets for the last of my own coins to pay for the juice and some time online. As I did a few strands of hair got in my face. I brushed them away, not realising they had snagged on the pack strap. When I straightened my head too quickly the wig yanked off and flopped onto the counter like a dead cat.

'Oops,' said Matt.

My face grew hot. I couldn't look at him. Inside I was furious at myself. Who needed a police search when I was so good at bungling my own disguise? Snatching the wig off the counter, I fled to the rest room.

When I had pulled myself together – hair on, tomato face faded – I went to get my drink, trying to pretend nothing had happened. Luckily Matt was busy with another order and had his back to me. I put the coins down and took the can, pulling the tab and glancing out through the big front window of the café as I went to take my first sip. What I saw made my hand freeze in mid-air. A white SUV was pulling into the parking lot.

*Go. Go. Go.*

I wanted to run, but the message wasn't reaching my legs. My body felt numb. I could only stare at the car licence plate letters. *SB*. *SB* for Slime Boys. *SB* for So Bad.

I recognised the camper-van guy immediately as he got out from the passenger side. Then the driver's door opened too. My stomach lurched. Ashtray man. I'd seen his eyes on the ferry, now I could see the rest. Red baseball cap, clipped brown hair, strong nose and jaw, that same hint of a sneer. Not tall, but top-heavy in the neck and shoulders. Like Uncle Dan's Hereford bull, the mean one that had to be put down.

*Hide!*

But the rest room was too close to the door – I'd never make it in time. Under a table? The café wasn't full; they'd see me and so would everyone else. The only other place within range was the counter. Would Matt betray me? There was only one way to find out. Glancing around to make sure no one was looking, I ducked down out of sight.

'Number sevent—' Matt was calling out an order number when he turned. The sight of me hiding below the cash register nearly made him drop the tray of burgers.

'Don't let them get me!' I begged.

I heard the café door open and knew the men were entering. Matt glanced across the room and must have put two and two together.

'Number seventeen!' he called out again.

Someone came over to collect the tray. 'And three Cokes, please,' I heard a woman say. Matt reached past me into the fridge.

I was hunched down, tensed like a hare ready to bolt. The woman moved away and after a moment a different voice, one with low menace in it, said, 'I'm looking for a kid and a horse. My daughter. Hair this long, dark. Brown pony with white socks. You seen her?'

Matt shook his head. 'Sorry, mate.'

I heard something being slid across the counter. 'Sure?'

Matt stared at whatever had been put there and shrugged. 'Wish I could help.'

The man ordered two coffees. Matt started preparing them, but the machine was out of coffee beans and he had to go to the storeroom for a new bag.

'Well?' I heard the SUV guy say in a low voice when he'd gone. 'See her anywhere?'

The camper-van driver answered, 'Nah, she's not here.' He paused. Then, worried: 'You reckon we can change the handover time? Bring the money a day later?'

'Sure, we'll ask them real nice. With flowers.' I could practically hear the SUV man's lip curl. 'Wake up, Ratch – this is the big game. We don't show, we're out.'

'Yeah, but what if we don't find her?'

'We'll find her.' The voice was hard. 'I've got too much pinned on this deal to let a brat on a nag mess it up. Or a driver who can't lock a van,' he added viciously. 'You better hope she turns up, and fast.'

'I-it was a mistake, Mason,' the camper-van driver – Ratch – stammered, adding quickly, 'What do we do with her after? And the horse?'

'Do?' said the one called Mason. 'We take care of business, that's what.'

My heart was doing triple time. I was a hair's breadth from being caught. I had left the pack on a chair by the wall and now I got the crazy notion that they would see the money inside, glowing like radiation. Most of all I prayed Tooth wouldn't wander into view.

Matt came back. He made the coffees. The men paid. After what seemed like forever the café door slammed and he murmured, 'They're gone.'

I let the breath I'd been holding out and slumped down onto the floor.

'Is he really your dad?' Matt asked.

'No!' I looked up. 'Thanks for not ratting.'

Matt pulled a face. 'He tried to buy me off! Jerk.'

'Well, thanks. You saved me. Really.'

He grinned. 'I owed you.'

I stared, not getting it.

'The mowing, remember?'

'Oh. Right.' I laughed. Some more of the adrenalin went out of me.

'Hey, are you OK?' he asked suddenly.

'I-I'm fine.' Matt seemed nice. It would have felt good to tell him what was going on. But I couldn't. I was getting ready to launch into one of my elastic truth specials to throw him off the scent when a man came up to put in an order. I made the most of it to slip into an empty computer booth and go online.

Maybe I couldn't tell Matt about the mess Tooth and I

were in, but I had to tell *some*body. 'We take care of business,' Mason had said. It didn't take a star IQ to guess what he'd meant. I knew that if he and his stooge caught up with us, they wouldn't let me go. I'd seen their faces and could identify them. And if we really did disappear, no one would ever know what had happened to us.

I got onto Ben's website and read his latest post. Nui was gone. He was pretty sure she'd migrated to breed. I left another note. I didn't want him to raise the alarm right away – we still had Mum's ashes to get to the Cape and everything might go fine. I just wanted to leave clues pointing to Mason and Ratch for him to figure out in case we did come to harm. I wrote:

**Holly**

Kia ora Ben, guess what? Me and my clever friend are going to watch Nui swim past the *last lighthouse* on her way to Tonga. If you don't hear from me, blame it on two supermaggots called Mason and Ratch (white SUV tagged SB).

We had to leave. Matt had seen my real hair, and by now the ID photos going around would be less Heidi and more Folly. I wanted to check the latest news reports online, but when I glanced towards the counter Carol had come back and Matt was talking to her. I was afraid it might be about me. I snuck out while they weren't looking.

# 15

We pushed hard all the way to the turn-off. It was under an hour to get there, but every second we spent on the state highway was dangerous. The men knew about the money and were out to get us. Right now they'd be scouting every road out of Awanui. If they came north we were toast.

Tooth kept up a steady trot and cantered whenever the verges were wide enough. The clouds raced with us. Telephone wires looped from pole to pole, marking the distance.

Once we'd turned onto the side road to the coast we could breathe a little easier. I part-unfolded the map in front of me.

'Hey, there's a Lake Carrot.'

'What about a fresh spring?' asked Tooth.

He was right to think about water. I had filled the bottles

at the café, but they wouldn't last us both long. When we saw a fat little piebald mare grazing in a field his ears pricked up. A horse meant a trough.

'Ask here,' he said, giving the mare an interested glance.

Tooth enjoys company. During our first year together he kept on at me to get him a field buddy, but the only time I ever mentioned it Mum made choking noises and Dad gripped the edge of the bench as if I'd gut shot him, which meant we couldn't afford it.

I looked at the farmhouse. Maybe he was right and I should risk it. Who knew when he'd get the next chance to drink.

I dismounted and we entered the property. The garden was tidy, with buzz cut hedges and a carport with a ping pong table. A tethered sheep was chewing a circle on the lawn.

The farmer had his head in a tractor engine not far from

the house, but as we got nearer a dog started barking and he looked up and saw us.

'Settle down, Bob!' he yelled at the dog. Then to me, friendly: 'What can I do for you, young lady?' He had a creased pink face with no-nonsense blue eyes and a white patch on his nose where some skin had been taken off.

'We were just going to the beach but, um, would it be OK if my horse had a drink at your trough first?'

The man grinned. 'Bit of a guzzler, is he?' He gestured towards a gate leading to the field. 'Go right ahead. Bonnie likes visitors.'

'Thank you.' I had started to move away when he stopped me with another question.

'Not going for a swim on your own, were you?'

I shook my head. 'Just a ride.'

'Good. The surf's tricky here – people get in trouble all the time. You from these parts?'

'I'm staying with my uncle.'

'Do I know him?'

'Dan Glover,' I said, easy as butter. Never mind that Uncle Dan's surname was Harris and he lived hours away.

I could see the farmer's brain ticking. Finally he gave up. 'Name's new to me.'

'Well, thank you for the water,' I said, hoping he'd stop quizzing me.

'If you're thirsty yourself the wife's bound to have something cold in the fridge.'

'No thank you, I'm fine.'

He gave a shrug. 'It's there if you change your mind.'

After I'd said thank you but no thank you again he told me, 'Once your horse has tanked up you can go out through the bottom gate. Gets you almost onto the beach. Mind the traffic.'

I smiled politely at the joke and we moved off. I could feel his eyes on my back. When I mentioned it to Tooth he said,

'That's because we look rare.' He meant not normal, and it was true. My wig was a knotty mess and sweat had turned his white socks into stripes. It was just as well we were making tracks.

The farmer was right about Bonnie – she was a good-natured sort. Not that I talked to her myself. I can communicate with Tooth, but it still doesn't work with other horses. Not long after he came along, I made a fool of myself finding that out when I tried to chat with a draft horse at the Dargaville Easter Show. First it stared down its nose at me, then it showed me its huge brown rump. Tooth laughed really hard when I told him.

'What's so funny? All he had to do was say hello.'

'Why? What was in it for him?'

'Friendship?'

'Did he look lonely?'

'Not really. But neither did you when I met you.'

'That's different. I was bored.'

His reply got me worried. If he felt bored again would he leave me for the next person who dangled a carrot in front of his nose? I couldn't bear the thought of it. My life would be over without him.

I had to know. A few days later while I was brushing the mud off his coat I asked him, 'Tooth, do you like me?'

'Sure.'

'I mean *really*. Like a best friend.'

'You're not a horse.'

'Well you're not a person and you're still *my* best friend.' I started working on his belly.

He was silent. Then: 'Thank you. I know that means a lot to you.'

The conversation wasn't going the way I'd hoped.

'Wouldn't you feel bad if we were separated?'

'Of course. We're used to each other now.' He blew out

through his nostrils as if that was all he was prepared to say on the matter. After a moment he added: 'A little more to the left, please.'

Sand. Then a frill of white and three different blues. Ninety Mile Beach stretched on and on.

'At last,' said Tooth.

I was relieved too. It was simple now: just go north.

I thought the farmer had been joking about the traffic, but at low tide plenty of tour coaches used the beach as a highway. We were coming out from the dunes when a busload of tourists zoomed past on its way home.

I wanted to get well away from the road entry. When we stopped at last I pulled the wig off. I'd felt protected wearing it but hiding from Mason and Ratch was what mattered now. From here on Tooth was Tooth and I was Folly. I hid my stuff and the saddle and bridle and his halter too in the dunes, marking the spot with a piece of driftwood. It was getting late, but there was still time for a real ride.

'Like to get that dumb paint off your legs?' I asked him.

'Thought you'd never ask.'

I swung up and rode bareback. The beach was empty in both directions. Some low clouds split the sunlight into golden shafts that beamed down like a picture of heaven. Gulls and terns were dipping in the shallows for shellfish, dropping them from a height onto the sand.

Near the water Tooth broke into a canter. Grasping a twist of mane in my fingers I leaned forward and murmured, 'Let's go!' I felt his stride lengthen; as he picked up speed his neck stretched out, every muscle in his body rising to the thrill of the open space. His hooves thrummed faster and faster. We were moving as one, thundering along the hard sand, the wind whipping his mane and my hair. Seabirds wheeled up and sheared away around us as we pounded through the skimming waves. I closed my eyes and thought *Only this is real. Only this is true.* Sea tears sprayed my cheeks. I wanted to drown in the shining sky. I wanted to gallop forever with this freedom blazing inside me – on and on past the end of the world, to a place where nothing died and no one I loved would ever be lost to me again.

It would have been nice to fall asleep in a tent looking out over the waves, but the pop-up was gone and we were runaways, not tourists. I found a hollow in the dunes set back from the beach and we had dinner: alfalfa pellets I'd found in the supermarket for Tooth, canned spaghetti for me. The cold spaghetti was slimy and gross. I couldn't finish it. As I slid into my sleeping bag Tooth wandered off to look for a patch of grass that wouldn't bung up his insides with sand.

'Stick to the dunes,' I said.

'Yes, Boss.'

A cool sea breeze had skimmed the heat off the sand hills. I propped the cylinder on the sand next to me as usual and as I was lying there curled up in a ball, eyelids about to close, Mum came to me. I saw her crouched a few metres away.

'What is it, Mum?' I asked, remembering what Kiri had said about wairua enjoying a chat with the living. 'You can tell me if something's wrong. I'll take care of it.'

A shadow passed over her face, like at the hospital when Dylan would stomp his foot and tell the doctors to hurry up and make his mummy *better*. Seeing her with that look brought back a whole lot of memories. Not good ones. Suddenly everything I'd been carrying hurt too much – a terrible ache I didn't know how to ease. Big, hiccuping sobs rose in my chest. I curled up even tighter and cried and cried into my sleeping bag.

When I'd cried the ache to a sniffle, she was still there.

'Soon we'll get to the Cape and I'll do the ashes thing,' I said. 'Is that all right?' I worried that it might not be what she wanted at all. But her expression didn't change. I took that as a yes.

I started telling her about everything that had happened since Tooth and I had set off. In case she'd missed parts. I even told her about the money and asked what I should do. She didn't answer, though she didn't disappear so fast this time either. I thought maybe Kiri had been right and she did like me talking to her. But I was so tired it got harder and harder to stay awake. She was still watching over me when my eyelids fell shut. It was a good, safe feeling.

# 16

When I woke next morning a seagull had its beak in the spaghetti. I'd overslept. I shouted at the gull and it flapped away. The can rolled down the dune.

It was a dull day with some heavy clouds shouldering in.

'Tooth,' I called, wriggling out of the sleeping bag and shaking sand out of the bag and my hair. 'Tooth?'

He didn't answer. I started muttering to myself about him holding us up, which wasn't really fair when I was the one who'd slept in. Then I climbed the sand slope to look for him.

No dark silhouette broke the long curves of the dunes. I left the gear heaped in a pile where I could see it and started stumping around looking for him, getting into a mood to match the clouds. He knew the plan, why couldn't he stick to it? He was probably on one of his grass missions. At this rate it would take a month to get to the Cape.

I finally saw him on the beach, being led back towards Awanui by two hump-backed figures with walking poles.

'Hey!' I started running. 'Hey!'

The wind snatched my words away. I kept running, calling out again and again until at last Tooth heard me and whinnied in reply. The walkers finally saw me too and stopped.

I caught up, panting.

'The horse is from you?' one of the women asked. Her face was button-round. The other woman was stringy, with hair pulled back so tight it made her eyes bulge. They were both carrying big backpacks.

'Yes!'

'There was a fish line on his huf,' said the button-faced woman.

'Hoof,' said her friend.

Button-face pointed to a small cut on Tooth's left fore

coronet. 'We have take it off. He was a good still boy.' She patted his neck. 'What is his name?'

'Sparky.'

Tooth looked insulted and stamped a hoof. I ignored him.

'We thought he is lost. We take him to the camping place.'

I gave Tooth a hard stare. 'Not lost, just late.'

The woman smiled and patted him again. 'Good Sparky.' She slipped something onto her palm and Tooth snuffled it up. 'In Austria I have also a horse,' she told me. 'A Holsteiner, that is a very old brood.'

'Breed,' said her friend.

'Yes, breed.'

They had been leading Tooth with a belt. Now Buttonface slipped it off. 'Sea washing, that is good. Of the huf – *ach nein*, hoof.'

Her friend nodded.

'Thanks, I'll do that.' I took hold of Tooth's halter. 'It was really nice of you to help, but we have to go.'

'Please, one moment.' The stringy woman pulled out her phone.

Great, a photo. I moved my head on purpose to blur it.

'We really have to go now,' I said, pulling Tooth away. 'Bye.'

'Sparky??' he said in disgust when we were far enough away.

'Was I supposed to tell them your real name? What happened?'

'I got tangled up. Silly me.'

I checked the cut. 'Why didn't you call out?'

'I did. You didn't hear.' He looked smug. 'They gave me a banana. I would have headed back sooner but I was angling for seconds.'

'I'll buy you a hundred bananas if we can just get to where we're going. We said to stay away from the beach, remember?'

'I know. But I smelled . . .' He lifted his head, nostrils keen. 'There was a herd. I went to see.'

'You mean wild?'

He nodded. I hadn't known about any free horses roaming up north. There was a look in Tooth's eye that suddenly made me wonder what he would have done if he'd found them.

I went to recover the gear and we set off. The pack was getting lighter as we used up the food, which was good or bad depending on whether we got tired or hungry. There was even enough room for the sleeping bag.

We kept away from the beach. For a few hours the tide would still be out far enough to drive on the sand and that meant buses and cars, maybe even the white SUV. My insides did a little flip whenever I thought about it. If the men were still looking for us – and in my heart I knew they were – I hoped they'd think we'd taken the sea route. The map showed a parallel road skirting the forestry land behind the dunes, so we cut across to find it.

It was dull on the back road, all grassy sand on one side and pine trees on the other. But it was quiet – we only saw one tractor the whole time. Even better, there was a campground. A sign said *Horses for beach trekking*, so there had to be water, too.

The horses were in a paddock with some sheep not far from the road. I could see a house, which meant people inside it might be able to see *me*, but I had to take that chance. I climbed over the wire fence with the folding bucket, snuck over to the trough and filled it. I tried to hurry back but that only made the bucket bang against my leg and half the water spill out.

'More please,' said Tooth when he'd drunk it dry, so I made another trip.

The horses were all ignoring Tooth, except for one big-boned, unfriendly-looking grey gelding who went over to check him out as I was returning. First he sniffed him. Then without warning he gave a quick, high flick with his foreleg as though he would have liked to strike him if the fence hadn't been in the way. He thrust out his muzzle to bite, but Tooth pulled back in time and retreated a short distance. Satisfied, the grey sauntered off.

'What was all that about?' I asked when I got back with the second half-bucketful.

'He was showing me my standing line.'

'I thought horses liked company,' I said.

'We do,' said Tooth, 'but with rules.'

'What kind of rules?'

'Keep space between, wait to be invited in – things like that.'

'He's got plenty of space! And it's not his field. He's not even a stallion.' I felt annoyed for Tooth's sake that the grey had been so rude.

Tooth didn't seem put out himself. 'In a day or two he'd let me share breath.'

'That's no use. We'll be gone.'

'It's no use anyway. I don't want to share breath with him.'

I told him it reminded me of school.

'You share breath?'

'No, I mean there are a few kids I get on with – *used* to get on with – and others I avoid.' It was weird to think my school days were over. A pity, too: just when my 'What I Did in the Holidays' essay could have slayed the competition. 'Actually, there was nobody I was getting on with lately,' I confessed.

'Sometimes paddocks sour that way.' Tooth turned his attention to the water I had brought him and guzzled it down with pleasure.

'Better?' I asked, stroking his neck.

'Better.'

I mounted. 'Leaving now,' I called out to the grey as we went away. Tooth's head was high, even a little haughty.

By the time we got back to the beach the tide had gobbled up most of the hard sand. It was slower walking on the soft stuff than on the forest road, but at least for a while there was no fear of anyone hunting us down. The sea and the salt zing in the air put a big feeling in my heart. Nothing from here to Australia! I kicked my feet out of the stirrups and started wheeling my arms round, singing at the top of my voice. Tooth nickered along. Or snickered.

After a while I jumped down and walked barefoot beside him, feeling the sand ooze up between my toes. Clouds bunched into shapes overhead. I made out a claw hand, a rhino, a gondola and a frozen chicken. Tooth saw salt licks.

'Hey Tooth, what did one ocean say to the other?' I asked him.

'Oceans talk?'

I sighed. 'You're meant to say "what".'

'What, then.'

'Nothing, they just waved.'

He snorted down his nose. I didn't mind – the funny stuff we tell each other doesn't always shoot for the same mark. The punchline of a joke he once told me went something like 'Two rabbits hopping in a twisty wind'. I didn't get it at all.

I tried one of Ben's. 'What do you call a dog magician?'

'What.'

'A labracadabrador.' That got a chuckly nicker. 'Your turn.'

He couldn't think of any just then, so we played Best Drink instead. Mine was cold lemonade. Tooth's was his own dam's milk.

'What did she look like?' I'd told him a lot about my mother, but he hardly ever spoke about his.

'Can't remember. I know what it felt like when she was there and when she wasn't. One day she wasn't.'

'Did someone buy you?'

He gave a shake of his head. 'The farmer came to the paddock with his dog. He caught my dam first and then he set the dog barking and yipping at my heels, getting in between us. She kicked out and whinnied for me to stay by her side, but I was too frightened. I bolted.'

'What then?'

'By the time I turned back they were already taking her away. I called out and galloped as fast as I could to reach her, but before I could make it, the gate had shut. All that day and the next and the next I kept calling out for her, but she never answered. They'd taken her to another part of the farm. The old nanny mare in my paddock told me I'd been *weaned*.' He made a strange horse noise – the kind he tells me I'll never understand.

'I'm sorry,' I said.

'Not your fault. Besides, I got over it.'

'Did you ever see her again?'

'Sure, many times. But it was never the same. Something was broken. And by the next spring she had a new foal to nurse.'

'But in real life . . . I mean in a herd, wouldn't she have had another foal anyway?'

'That's right. She would have driven me away.'

'So . . .' I hesitated, not wanting to say the wrong thing.

'So what difference?' He thought for a moment. 'It was between me and my dam. That farmer had no business.'

I remembered his words when the wild horses appeared at sunset, not far from where I'd set up for the night.

There was nothing cosy about camp now – without the pop-up it was just the place where I unrolled the sleeping bag and dumped the saddle. Mum's shimmer didn't turn up and I wasn't tired enough to fall straight to sleep. I sat hunched and miserable, hugging the cylinder and trying not to let the hard seed of aloneness inside me grow. Out here in the open dunes it wasn't exciting to be on my own. There was too much sky. The sea washed on and on. I felt smaller than a sand flea.

Tooth said nothing, but he sensed my mood and stayed nearby, pretending to find new bits of grass to munch. It meant everything that he was there.

I leaped to my feet when they came: eight horses galloping as one over the dunelands, close but never colliding, weaving a sure path through the marram. They looked wild to the core.

On a sandy ridge overlooking the sea they stopped. They were lean and unkempt, but the light put a bronze and copper sheen on their coats and sparked their long manes and tails. For a moment they stayed that way, their fine heads turned seawards. I suddenly had the thought that Tooth could have been one of them, and felt sad he'd never had a chance at real freedom.

He whinnied to them. The herd leader's ears pricked, alert. His answer rang out bugling and proud, before he wheeled away and plunged down the dune towards the forest, the others thundering fast on his heels.

Together we watched them go. When the last horse had vanished into the pines I said, 'Tooth, do you ever wish—'

'No.'

He came and rested his velvety muzzle on my shoulder. I stroked his nose. We stayed that way for a while, both of us quiet. His answer had come too fast to be true, but I loved him for it anyway.

# 17

I thought the hard sand would be easier going, but Tooth said after a while it hurt his legs, so next morning we mostly stuck to the shallows. We had set off early, the sun only just up. I wanted to beat the buses and cover some distance.

The beach was endless. I tried to find markers – anything to break it up. There were shells as big as my hand, a half-eaten baby shark and some little jellyfish like blue glass strewn along the waterline.

'Keep a lookout,' I told Tooth. 'Sometimes containers fall off ships and break open, or people just find things.'

'What things?'

'Like trainers and whiskey and stuff. Once, this huge eyeball washed up.'

Tooth only dipped an ear. It would take more than an eyeball to get him worked up. Later I saw a biggish dark shape on the sand up ahead, but it was only a hump of seaweed.

Before the first buses came we headed for the back road again. It wasn't just that we had to lie low; Tooth needed food. Tough sea grass and snatched mouthfuls weren't enough any more.

'There's a hole as big as a barn in my gut,' he grunted.

I was hungry as well, but I had biscuits to snack on and raisins and cheese from the supermarket. I'd bought more oats for Tooth, too, but when I suggested them he said, 'I want a full meal under my feet.'

Finally we found a good long stretch of pasture by one of the forestry roads running inland. I unsaddled him and heaped our things out of sight between some trees, figuring we might as well stay there for a bit. While Tooth filled up I could nap on my sleeping bag in the shade. I'd had a bad night with all sorts of weird dreams and the midday sun and wind were frazzling my brain. When I'd made my packing list I'd forgotten about a hat.

'If anyone comes, slip into the forest,' I told him. 'They'll think you're wild.'

He gave a little snort as if the idea tickled him, then put his head down for some serious feeding.

The sound of dirt bikes and hooting and a frightened whinny woke me a couple of hours later. At first I thought I was having another bad dream, but then I blinked awake and jumped up. Something was wrong.

Shapes were flashing in and out of the trees. It took me a moment to understand what was going on. Two riders were chasing Tooth, revving their bikes to herd him forward, driving him in circles and skidding round to block his way when he tried to veer off.

'Giddy-up, gee-gee!' shouted the rider on the blue bike.

'Yee-ha!' screeched the other one, swinging his arm as if he had a lasso and laughing like the whole thing was hilarious.

Even from a distance I could see the panic in Tooth's movements. He was going to hurt himself. He almost ran straight into a trunk to avoid one of the bikes.

'Leave him alone!' I screamed. I started sprinting through the trees. I was so mad. I was going to smash their stupid bikes to pieces.

At last the one on the blue bike noticed me.

'Stop it, you're frightening him!' I shouted.

The rider's helmet visor was up. I could see him laughing at me, a pipsqueak kid bawling him out for hassling her pony. *New fun*, he must have thought. Leaving Tooth to his mate, he swung his bike round to face me squarely. Then he flicked his visor down, gave a few loud revs and rode straight at me.

I checked, startled. He was joking . . . wasn't he? But the

motorbike kept coming, faster and faster. I gulped. My legs were suddenly useless. The rider was hunched over the handlebars, leaning into the speed. At the last minute he pulled the bike up into a wheelie and powered towards me on his rearing mount. I screamed. My hands flew up in front of me and I looked away, waiting for the crash.

He sped past so close I felt the brush of his jacket sleeve on my arm. A moment later his friend zipped by a short distance away. Sprays of dry needles and dirt churned up from their back wheels as they zoomed off along a track leading coastwards, their laughter hanging in the air with the exhaust fumes. Then it grew quiet.

Tooth's sides were heaving and he was lathered in sweat. I hurried to him and ran my hands over his neck and flank.

'Easy now. Easy. They're gone,' I told him, and myself. My hands were trembling.

He stood there listening, letting me soothe him.

'What happened?' I asked when we were both calmer.

'Nothing, they saw me. I did like you said but they followed. They wanted to make me run.'

I always feel terrible when Tooth tells me about nasty things people do, as though it's partly my fault. 'I'm sorry,' I said. 'If I hadn't been sleeping . . .'

He nudged me to be quiet. 'They were just bad ones.'

I packed up and we set off again. Tooth was sorry to leave the grazing.

'There was a good bit down the end . . . some leaf I've never tasted before . . .'

I meant to take the first path that would get us back onto the sand, so we could make the most of the high tide. But as we were going through the dunes I spotted two dirt bikes, one blue and the other white, parked almost at the entrance to the beach.

It was them.

'Quick – back up!' I told Tooth. When we were out of sight I jumped down and led him to a spot where he couldn't be seen. 'Wait here for me.'

He gave me a look. 'What are you—?'

'Nothing. Just stay put.'

I scooted up over the dunes, keeping low. When I was near the beach I got down on my belly and crawled closer.

I nearly came out on top of them. They were sniggering and carrying on about something.

'Woah, that much? You wanna fly us to China?'

'Nah, just Sydney, hahaha.'

Through a clump of marram I saw one of them trying to roll a smoke while the other did a useless job of sheltering him from the wind. Good. It would keep them busy.

I slithered backwards and ran to where the bikes were parked. First, I uncapped all the wheel valves. Next, I unscrewed the metal ring things. Then I used one of the points on Kiri's keepsake to push the pin in each valve. The tyres were a lot fatter than bicycle wheels and it was really satisfying to hear all that air hissing out. Giddy-up. Yee-ha.

Once the tyres were good and flat I arranged the valve bits into a smiley face on one of the seats. Then I went to get Tooth.

'Let's try the next track,' I said, and climbed back in the saddle. When I told him what I'd done he broke into a canter, light as the breeze.

We were lucky; there was a trickle of fresh water near the place where we stopped that evening. I hoped it was our last night on the sand. I'd had it with gritty sleeping bags and I'd had it with windy shores and I never wanted to see another can of cheesy macaroni in my life.

After we'd pitched camp I gave Tooth a proper brushing down, going over every inch. Back when I thought that knowing all the facts in the world about ponies was the secret to finding one, I used to say the horse parts out loud to remember them. Even later on I did it sometimes when I was grooming Tooth. He thought it was funny. 'Where are my feathers again?' he'd ask, and 'What's a fetlock?' 'Chestnut' always got him hawing.

Afterwards while I was shining the torch on the map, a big fat beetle swooped down over my head. I screamed and started hopping about in my sleeping bag like I was in a sack race, batting it away with one hand and holding the bag up with the other.

Tooth came trotting over, but when he saw what the fuss was about he just stared at me.

'What? Well how would *you* like it in *your* mane?'

The beetle was lying upside down on the sand, wiggling its legs. I flipped it back over. It was one of those really shiny bumbly ones that are actually pretty cool except when they're tangled in your hair. If I'd had my phone I would have taken a picture for Ben's blog.

'Don't you ever eat insects by mistake?' I asked Tooth once I was settled again. The wind had quieted and it was peaceful.

'Sometimes there are crunchy parts, yes,' he said.

'Ew.' I shuddered, imagining the cracking sound. 'Don't you mind?'

'The grass is brighter.'

'What?' He was coming in horseways again.

'Crunchy bits help the shine.'

I clicked. At least I thought I did. 'You mean like fertiliser.'

'Like dead bones,' he said. 'Like river run. Like foal play.'

'*Foal* play?'

He blew his lips, not in the mood to explain. 'Anyway, insects that bite *me* are worse. Horseflies. I once saw a mare jump a five-bar gate almost from a standstill when a horsefly bit her. They really sting. It's why I roll in mud sometimes. Keeps them off me.'

'And I get to brush it all off. Thanks.'

'You'd do the same.'

'Actually, I hear there's this thing called a tail? Lucky yours is nice and long to swish them away.'

'And my mane. To cover my neck.'

In the darkness I grinned.

'And your mane.'

# 18

Next day on the back road we took a wrong turning that led away from the beach. By the time I'd noticed I couldn't hear the surf any more we'd already been off track for a while. I didn't want to go all the way back. The small roads weren't on my map, but I thought it wouldn't be too hard to find a path to the coast again.

An hour later we were still going around in circles. Tooth would have had plenty to say about it at the start of the trip, but neither of us had the energy for bickering any more. The only good thing was that along the way we found a small water hole. It looked cloudy to me, but he said the taste was all right. I was glad I still had the bottles to drink from.

We were coming away from the hole when a farmer riding

a dusty quad bike with a sheepdog perched on the back came zipping along the track. The space wasn't wide and he had to slow the bike down to a crawl to pass us.

He raised a hand in greeting. With no wig disguise any more I was worried about being recognised so I gave a quick little answering smile and glanced away. But we must have been doing a good job of looking lost, because instead of driving on he stopped.

'You two managing all right there?'

'Um, could you please tell us how to get to the beach?' I asked. 'I think we took the wrong track.'

He grinned. He had a cheery round face. A black baseball cap was turned backwards on his head. His old green shirt had a frayed hole in the pocket and his shorts and gumboots were as dusty as the bike.

'Sure did – this one goes up to Te Kao. Just tuck in behind me and I'll show you the turn-off.'

He drove slowly so the bike wouldn't lift dust in our faces.

‘Heading for Te Paki?’ he called over his shoulder.

‘Yes.’

‘Bit of a hike on your own, isn’t it?’

He wasn’t asking in a prying way, but straight away I tensed. We were so close to our goal now – it would be terrible if he suddenly realised who we were and our whole long trek came to nothing!

‘I’m, uh, meeting my friend.’

‘Nice one! Have a slide for me. Back in the day me and my mates used to go camping up there and race each other down the dunes on bits of cardboard. It was mean! That’s where I lost this.’ He grinned and pulled at the corner of his mouth to show the gap of a missing tooth.

I stared. How could anyone do that on a sand dune?

‘Not sand,’ he said, guessing my thoughts. ‘One time my brother Wiremu cut me off near the bottom and I slammed into his elbow.’ He chuckled. ‘Hated losing, that Wiri. You got brothers and sisters?’

'One brother.'

'Better watch out, then.'

'Mine's not like that. And he's younger than me.'

'Yeah, Wiri was a cute little bunny once too.' The farmer chuckled again. 'When you least expect it, expect it.'

As we went on he kept up a friendly patter. Just farm stuff mostly, and nothing nosy about me. I relaxed a bit, only half-paying attention. He'd gotten me thinking about Dylan, and suddenly I had to swallow hard, remembering how sad his eyes had looked on the news. I missed him.

After about ten minutes we came to a small side track.

'Straight down there and right at the fork. Can't go wrong.' He wished me a good ride and zoomed off in a cloud of dust.

The tide wasn't right for us yet, but I didn't want to get lost on back roads again. We'd have to risk the beach.

'Or we could wait in the dunes until high tide,' I suggested to Tooth.

Neither of us really wanted that. Our food was too low to be wasting any time. Tooth had no more clue than me about what would happen once we reached the lighthouse, but now that he'd given up trying to make me turn back he wanted to get there as quickly as I did.

The late morning traffic was all heading north. Buses tooted, tourists waved.

'Bye, slowpokes!' shrieked a boy half-hanging out a passenger window, his laugh pulled away with the car.

Hour after hour, the long waves lifted and smashed. Tooth plodded on. The rhythm of his steps rocked me gently in the saddle. The further we went, the less we spoke. It was as if we'd gone past words, past everything. My mind was scoured bare. When I thought about Dad and the money trouble it was all a blur, an echo in a seashell.

As the tide rose, the beach emptied. Soon the only people

left were surfcasters using up the last of their bait. I asked a woman in a neon wind jacket if it was far to the giant dunes and she told me a couple more hours would get us there. It felt strange to be speaking to another person. My voice sounded rusty.

'Need a lift?' she joked, tossing her head at a pick-up backed up to the sand hills. 'You and Lightning there look pretty pooped.' Her brow furrowed. 'Don't I know you?'

My heart lurched. I pretended to think, before shaking my head. 'No, I don't think so.'

She wouldn't stop staring. I pointed to her rod. 'You've got a bite.'

It worked. Forgetting all about me, she hurried to attend to the line. I chirruped at Tooth to keep going.

'She knew about you,' he said when we were far enough away.

'Yeah, maybe I should whip us up a pair of seaweed wigs.'

'I don't fancy a crab in my ear.'

I tossed my head. 'Anyway, so what. We'll be gone before she remembers.'

Even though I was playing it down, I kept glancing over my shoulder. But the fishing must have been too good. No pick-up came after us.

Two hours is still a lot of beach. There was no galloping now – Tooth trudged on step after step. I was lost in my own thoughts.

My tummy rumbled. The rumbling got me thinking about food, which got me thinking about Mum's cooking. She was a terrible cook. Her cakes flopped. Her stews burned. She'd start on dinner and get distracted by something in the news, or Dylan and me singing in the bath, or the way a summer sunset turned our old shed roof the colour of persimmons. Next minute the smoke alarm would be screaming. Once, the neighbours called the fire brigade. Mum just laughed.

She had a great laugh, warm and throaty. 'New recipe,' she told the firemen. 'Want a taste?'

One time when it was cold and wet and Dylan was snivelling and I was bored she threw down her book and said, 'Right, time for the GPR.' We all went into the garden in the drizzling rain and put up the beach umbrella. Then, with a shovel and Dylan's toy spade we dug a small pit for a fire. While Dylan and I looked for three pointy sticks, she cut some potatoes really thin and when the embers were hot we roasted the slices and then slathered them in tomato sauce so they didn't burn our tongues. That was it: the Great Potato Recipe.

I kept scanning the beach for her wairua. A flicker would be enough, just a sign to know she was there with me. To keep me going. I'd been trying to pretend everything was still OK, but the further we went the more lost I was feeling. Not *lost* – I knew where we were going and how to get there – but inside I was starting to drift.

'Stop,' I told Tooth.

He pulled up. I slid the backpack round to rest on his withers and dug to the bottom. When my fingers found the cylinder with Mum's ashes I took it out. My windbreaker had a big zipped pocket on the front and I slid the cylinder inside. It hung against my chest like an anchor, reminding me why we were there. *We haven't forgotten you, Mum.* I patted my jeans pocket with Kiri's keepsake in it, too, for a bit of extra strength.

'OK, we can go again now.'

Tooth didn't ask what the stop had been for. He seemed just as busy with his own thinking as me. Maybe he was wondering how he'd wound up traipsing along Ninety Mile Beach with a supposed-dead girl thief when other ponies were in clover on farms, or being pampered at pony clubs, or even going through their dressage paces like Darcy. Maybe he was wishing he'd said no to my lunch carrot that day by the roadside.

The sun was setting when we finally reached the big dunes. I slid down out of the saddle and did a stiff little victory dance on the sand. Together we finished off the second bottle of water, and after a bit of searching I found one last peppermint and gave it to Tooth. As he slobbered away with minty dribble leaking from the corner of his mouth I leaned against his shoulder and stared at the darkening sweep of coastline, hardly believing we had travelled it. I tried to show him the distance on the map, but he wasn't interested.

'My hooves know how far.'

I twirled a strand of mane around my finger. 'Are you OK?'

He made a show of checking his legs. 'Still all there, so I suppose yes.'

'When we' – I nearly said 'get back' before I remembered there wasn't going to be any 'back' – 'when we find someplace to stop and rest, I'll make sure you have a ton of special feed. The best hay. Oats every day. Watermelon.'

'Feel free to throw in molasses. And you promised bananas.'

'You'll get fat.'

'Sounds fair.'

I looked around at the dunes. 'Shall we sleep here?' I didn't want to, but he should be the one to choose. He'd been carrying me all day.

'And eat this stuff again?' He meant the marram grass. 'It takes forever to chew. Plus sand.'

'You're just spoilt. Those other horses weren't complaining.'

'Did you look at them? I didn't see a lot of fat on the bone. And this is summer.'

I'd only been teasing, but it made me feel better to hear there was something about his own life that he actually preferred. Or maybe he was trying to make me feel good on purpose.

I did a bad job of hiding my relief. 'OK, we won't stop. Don't say you didn't have the chance.'

'Don't get me started on missed chances.'

Silver rivulets leaked out of the dunes onto the beach in

the dying light. The 'road' inland was actually a very shallow stream bed. Tooth's hooves kicked spray onto the toetoe bushes and other plants lining the banks.

It was nearly dark and I was dog tired. Part of me wanted to curl up somewhere – anywhere – and sleep for days, but the idea that we were so close to the end of the journey, the first one at least, gave me strength. All I had to do was keep going. I hugged the cylinder to me with one arm. *Soon, Mum. Soon.* I had it all figured out. Or I thought I did, until a white SUV came charging from behind the dunes.

# 19

The headlights were like a double punch; for a moment I was too stunned to react. Then real fear kicked in and I hauled Tooth around. 'Go!' I cried, giving him his head.

He sprang forward and bolted the way only an animal in danger can. This was no fun ride, no sunset gallop – we were being hunted. His legs moved like pistons, stream water shooting from under his hooves.

The SUV was forcing us seawards. On the beach there was plenty of hard sand to drive on. The car would easily outrace us. I had to get rid of the backpack – now. As we rounded a bend in the stream, thundering along by the bank, I slipped it off and let it drop into the bushes. I was looking everywhere for a way to get out of the car's path, but the banks were too high on one side and too tree-lined on the other.

The stream bed widened into the beach. I heard a crack, then another. Tooth gave a high-pitched scream and reared up. I was thrown. I landed hard on my side, the wind knocked out of me. Light glared. Car doors opened. Someone – the camper van driver – grabbed my arm and pulled me over.

'It's her! Different hair, but it's her, all right. And that's the horse – remember how I said about the mane . . .' He gripped my arm tighter. 'What'd you do with it, you little . . . We've got a load to—'

'Shut it, Ratch,' his partner snarled. Then to me: 'Where is it?'

In my mind I had gone over what I would say if I was caught. Tough, smart answers. Now I squeaked like a gerbil: 'Where's what?'

Ratch yanked my arm up behind my back. Pain knifed

through my shoulder and I cried out. From a short distance away Tooth whinnied in alarm.

Mason motioned Ratch to stop. He came closer and crouched beside me, a gun dangling on his finger. When he spoke his tone was even and he didn't lay a finger on me. He didn't have to – his eyes were boring into me like bullets.

'What's your name, girl?'

'M-Molly.'

'OK, Molly, the thing we're talking about here is cash. *My* cash. Which you seem to have decided was yours.' His voice grew even more dangerously soft. 'I call that stealing. And if there's one thing I can't stand, it's a thief . . .'

'I don't know about any money! I haven't taken anything!'

Mason sighed. His gaze travelled to Tooth. He aimed the gun. That was when I saw the bloodied graze along Tooth's rump and understood why he'd reared up.

'No! Don't hurt him!'

Mason shrugged. 'Your choice.' He glanced at his watch. 'For about three seconds.'

'It's in the pack!' I pointed miserably. 'The money . . . I dropped it somewhere back there.'

Ratch ran to look with his phone torch. A few minutes later there was an excited 'Got it!!' When he returned with the bag he ripped it open by force and shook the contents onto the sand. The money tumbled out along with the sleeping bag, a bunch of dirty clothes, cans of food and the rest. Ratch scrabbled through the mess for the banknotes. 'They're all here!' he told Mason once he'd counted the rolls. 'We're on!'

Mason squashed him fast. 'Not yet we aren't.' His meaty hand closed around my wrist. Hauling me to my feet, he put the gun under my nose to remind me what would happen if I tried to make a run for it, then shoved me in Tooth's direction. 'Get the nag.'

Tooth was standing at the edge of the darkness. Why hadn't he taken off when he'd had the chance? My thoughts were whirring crazy-fast as I walked towards him. Together we didn't stand a chance. I could never mount quickly enough and no half-pie escape gallop could match a gun. The best I could do was distract Mason and Ratch while he made a break for it. They'd worry about me before chasing a pony.

I didn't really want Tooth to go. The idea of being on my own was awful. A lump rose in my throat, but I squashed it down. I had to do this now. If I waited I'd lose my nerve.

'When I tell you, run,' I murmured once I was close enough to him, taking hold of a rein.

I turned back towards the men. Tooth was walking next to me on the side of the darkness and the sea. After a couple of steps I took a deep breath.

'Now.' At the same time I dropped the rein, threw myself down and started putting on a real show, crying and begging them not to hurt me. It began as an act to buy time for Tooth, but suddenly I was really feeling it. The more the reality of what was happening hit me, the more I worked myself up.

Mason had no time for it. 'Get her up,' he snapped at Ratch.

I was curled into a ball on the sand with my eyes clamped shut and my hands over my ears, trying to seal everything out. It didn't work. When Ratch set me roughly onto my feet the drone of the surf was still there and the headlights showed the same nightmare scene. Worst of all, Tooth hadn't budged. He was right beside me.

Mason went to the SUV and opened the hatch. He came back into the light holding a proper torch and a small shovel.

'Let's go.'

Ratch shoved me toward Tooth, pointing at the halter rope looped to the saddle.

'Gimme that.'

I passed the rope end to him. With Mason in front shining the torch, he half-pushed me and half-dragged Tooth up onto the lumpy dunes behind the beach.

It was hard to see where we were going. I kept stumbling

on the uneven sand. Each time, Ratch just pulled me up and onward. Further back from the beach we passed a low wooden hutch and then there was a dip in the sand and Mason said, 'Here.'

My heart started racing. This was it.

But it wasn't yet. Mason threw the shovel to Ratch.

'Dig.'

Ratch caught it, pulling a face. 'Aw jeez . . .'

'Don't "jeez" me!' Mason's eyes were savage in the torchlight. 'Do I have to spell it out again?' He started going on about a property deal gone wrong and how the cops were after them and other stuff I didn't understand. Then he said nastily, 'This number can set us both right, but instead of closing it we're out here getting sand in our socks, all because you couldn't do your job properly. Now *dig*.'

Ratch looked even more sour, but he didn't dare answer back.

'Teach you to lock up,' Mason sneered.

I was standing beside Tooth. Mason had us covered – he wasn't taking any chances. *It's a grave. They're going to bury us here.* Did Tooth understand what was happening? I had to dig my fingernails into my palms not to start crying again.

A message tone buzzed. Mason read the text on his phone and tapped out an answer right away, but the connection must have been bad, because he suddenly went into a rant about who the hell would ever want to live in the boonies with lousy coverage like this.

'It's them,' he told Ratch, his words clipped and tense. 'Something about the drop point. I need to find a high spot. You keep going here.'

'What about the girl? I can't dig and guard her and the horse at the same time!'

Mason swore and started flashing the torch about as if that might somehow fix the problem. I hoped someone passing would see the light and wonder what was going on. But at night on Ninety Mile Beach? Fat chance.

He wasn't waving the torch for nothing – it was the hutch he was searching for. When the beam lit on it he grabbed a handful of my windbreaker in his fist and marched me towards it, almost lifting me off the ground at each step. There was no padlock on the latch. He slid it open, tugged the door wide and gestured with the gun.

'Inside.'

I had to bend over to get in. The hutch was empty, but it smelled of fish. Someone must have used it to store gear. Mason slid the latch, locking me inside, and then Ratch slipped Tooth's halter rope around one of the wooden slats and tied it fast.

Why was Tooth being so tame? Back in Kiri's forest just the idea of a pig had been enough to make him bolt – what was stopping him now? I didn't get it.

I was mad at myself, too. *We knew this could happen, why didn't we work out a code? Headshake means bite, foot stamp means kick his guts out, nod means run like crazy . . .* We'd had a whole beach.

Mason left the big light with Ratch and used his phone torch to see by. Through the slats I could see him walking away. Ratch went back to the grave site and started shovelling sand. He was only a few steps away from us and I could hear him whinging and muttering under his breath about always having to do the grunt work.

I sat huddled against the side of the hutch, my face pressed to the wood. The scared feeling inside me grew and grew. I couldn't get past it. All I wanted was for the roof to fly off my cage. I wanted a hand to pluck us both out of there and set Tooth in his paddock and me at breakfast, with Dad making scrambled eggs and Dylan talking Wookiee. Dad would scoop the eggs onto the toast and say just like he did every time: 'Good enough for the king of Hunky Dory!'

But there was no paddock and no Dad and no Dylan. There was only the sound of the shovel, and the surf grinding on and on in the background. There was no hand.

‘Why didn’t you *run*?’ I sniffled miserably to Tooth. ‘You were supposed to get away.’

He didn’t answer. Instead he lowered his head so that his nostrils were close to the slats, right by my face. Then he breathed out.

It was like a warm puff of hope on my cheek. The fear shrivelled and my mind quieted enough for a space to clear. I stopped crying. Things were looking pretty terrible, but for now both of us were still all right. I sat up. We could get out of this mess. I had to think.

# 20

The scared feeling was still there, but while I had a grip on it I had to wear Ratch down. His hole wasn't going well. As fast as he could dig sand out, more would slide back in.

Putting on a bold voice, I said loudly, 'Might take a while.'

He didn't answer. As if to prove me wrong he started digging double fast, really putting his back into it. It was no good. The dry sand kept avalanching into the hole.

'You should try over there where there's grass.'

'Shut up.'

'It's true. The roots help stop the sand. We did a project at school. I got *very good-slash-excellent*.'

Ratch swore and carried on. But after a few more minutes

at it he slammed the shovel into the sand and straightened up. The hole was hardly deeper than his ankles.

'Nice one for a stingray.'

'I said SHUT UP!' Snatching the torch, he stomped over to a hollow in one of the grassier dunes and started again.

He had his back to us. I could see the flash of the shovel blade each time he threw sand over his shoulder. He'd stopped swearing, so I guessed things must be going better.

'See?' I called out, but he didn't bother to reply.

When I gave the word Tooth put his head down and started nibbling at the latch of the hutch with his lips and teeth. The pin was a bit stiff, but with some wriggling he managed to partly slide it. A little more wriggling and it was back all the way. Like I'd told Ben: good at gates.

I eased the door open and crept out. There was no need to untie Tooth's rope; I just unclipped it from his halter and quietly laid the clip on the sand. Ratch was still digging. He didn't hear a thing.

I couldn't see Mason's light, but he probably wasn't very far away. He might come back any moment. We crept away a few paces and then I let Tooth lead. He sees better than me in the dark. Once we'd gone a little further I mounted, and quiet as two sandhoppers we started towards the beach.

It went fine for a bit. Then Ratch must have glanced round and noticed Tooth was missing.

'Hey!'

I looked back and torchlight stabbed my eyes. A fraction later, from a higher mound to our left, Mason's phone beam shone.

'What the *hell* . . . Get her!' he shouted.

My fear shot through Tooth like electricity; on level ground he would have bolted. But even though the dunes were just low mounds and nothing like the rises we'd seen on the other side of the stream bed, the fastest he could go in the dark was a speeded-up amble. We had a head start on the men, but they had light to see. The two beams followed us like radars homing in on a target.

At last we reached the flat. Tooth didn't wait to be told – the second his hooves touched the beach he was off at a gallop. He did his best, but after a minute or two I heard the SUV growl to life, and before long the men had us in the headlights. The car ate up the distance between us. A few more seconds and we'd be in shooting range.

'The sea!' I cried to Tooth, and without breaking stride he veered for the water, splashing through the shallows. Then he was plunging into the dark waves, head high and straining, nostrils wide. His legs left the bottom and as he plunged through the battering surf a wave crashed against me. I swallowed seawater, gasping and sputtering for air. Before I could recover the next wave washed me right out of the saddle.

The shock of it stopped my breath. Swirling water engulfed me. I couldn't see. Flailing my arms, I tried to get back to Tooth, but my wet clothes and boots and the cylinder dragged me down. I went under, tumbled by the force of the water. Panic blurred everything. Where was up?

*Mum, help me!* My hand shot out and I felt myself being pulled up, undrowning. When my head broke the surface I drew gasping, sobbing breaths. My fingers were clamped around a hard metal stirrup. Somehow I managed to hang on as Tooth got us past the breakers.

The car headlights glared across the water. The men could see us, but we were out of range. Then we were past the lights, too. Tooth kept swimming in line with the land and I clung to the stirrup. If I was separated from him again I'd never make it to shore alone. I didn't want to think about how long he could hold out.

At last they gave up and the car headed back along the stream. They had their money back. Mason had talked about the 'drop point' and Ratch had mentioned a 'load' – were they going to pick it up?

Tooth made for shore. When his hooves struck ground I staggered out of the sea beside him and stood trembling on the sand in the dark. Crying and shaking with cold, my fingers numb, I lifted the saddle flap and undid the girth buckles. A waterlogged saddle was useless, a deadweight. I gave it a push and it dropped belly-up onto the sand.

I took out the cylinder. The wood was wet but the seal was still fine. My fingers could barely hold it while I tried to jump onto Tooth's back. I was so weak it took me four tries, but I managed at last. Then I zipped the cylinder back into the windbreaker pocket and we set off along the stream bed. The torch and the map were gone. We didn't need them – there was one road north and no going back. The chilly night breeze cut to the bone. I lay forward and pressed myself against Tooth's skin for heat. I could barely see a thing. Only the quiet splashes of his hooves told me we were headed the right way.

It was a small sound. Tooth suddenly tensed and pulled up short, so I heard it too: a car door being opened. A charge of terror and adrenalin went through me. *They're here.* Then car lights blasted us again. As Mason morphed from the shadows and came forward, the gun outlined in his hand, my fingers crept to the pocket of my jeans.

'Get off the horse.' His face was masked with cold rage. When I didn't react he strode forward and clamped a hand on my arm. 'I said—'

I lashed out, Kiri's tin keepsake clenched tightly in my fist. Its jagged edge slashed across his face and he bellowed with pain and fury. One hand went to his eye. A shot blasted from the gun in his other hand, barely missing me.

I was too shocked to move. Tooth was too brave or startled not to. Wheeling on his haunches, he leaped away out of the headlight glare and started labouring up the bank in the dark. I hung on – just.

Mason fired again wildly, shouting to Ratch, 'Get the

lights on them, you fool! I can't see them. They're getting away!'

Tooth's hooves were sinking deep in the sand and each breath came heavy as he battled to keep a footing. There was another sharp crack and he faltered, then struggled on. When I heard the car engine revving a sob escaped me. They would see us. Mason would shoot. We would die on a sandbank in the dark.

Again and again Ratch gave the engine gas. The headlights stayed fixed. There was a sound of wheels spinning.

'It's sunk in. The bloody thing won't move!' Ratch's voice rose over the noise of the motor just as Tooth finally crested the bank. Mason raged. We didn't wait around to hear more.

'Find the road,' I gasped. I was afraid we'd get lost in the dunes. The reins hung slack on Tooth's neck. It was up to him; I had no way to help.

I was hunched over and shivering, frozen through. Even when my wind jacket dried, the clothes underneath stayed clammy and damp, sealing in the cold. The chattering of my teeth mixed with the crunch of Tooth's hooves on gravel. *He did it*, I realised in a daze. Somehow he had looped around to the road.

I never thought to ask for help. There were farmhouses, but dogs barked us away. Porch lights glowed out of reach. Tooth and I were outcasts; we didn't belong in that world any more. Maybe not *any* world – everything felt far away and unreal. In my mind only the lighthouse beacon shone bright, the last place left for us to go.

We reached the state highway. A truck flew around the bend, slinging headlight glare, and Tooth pulled back in fright. I only just clung on in time.

'That way.' I guided him with a press of my leg.

We met no other cars. There were no lights and barely a

moon, but Tooth's step was steady and sure on the asphalt. It began to rain – just enough to soak us through again. After a while the wind died and the sky settled.

The even *tloc tloc* of hooves and the rocking movement lulled me. Time unwound: I was six and Mum and Dad were swinging me between them, lifting me higher and higher. I was eight: Dad racing me around the house and Mum and Dylan cheering me on from the porch. Nine: Auntie Nora cooking breakfast, Mum in hospital. Still nine: Tooth cantering towards me across the foggy winter paddock. Ten: Mum sitting on my bed, telling me she was going back in for more tests.

*But they said!*

*I know, and now they want to make sure.*

*What if they find it again? Mum, I'm scared.*

'Did you say something?' asked Tooth, or maybe he didn't. I think I shook my head. He kept walking.

I was shivery and burning up at the same time, slumped

over with tiredness. The dark crushed my shoulders. The stars were prickly burrs. I wanted to shrug it all off and sleep. But if I dozed and fell off now I'd never have the strength to climb back on.

'Tooth?'

'Yes.'

'Please talk to me.'

And he did. Not in humanspeak – it was the other sounds he used, the ones as old as the world of horses. Half-feverish, I listened. He told me about fields of sweet grass tickled by a soft, lucky breeze, a place where the stream burbles and there's a time to listen and another to turn away. He said the air tightens before a storm, but after rain colours travel well. Secrets underfoot don't last, he said, and need swiftness to be read. He told me some trees are generous with their shade, others hold back, and that when birds sing of distance their songs are always true.

The slow tattoo of his hooves held me in a trance. My fingers were crabbed around two clumps of mane – if I let go

I would fall. It began to spit again, but I was past caring. Waves of fire swept through my body, then a deep, shuddering cold.

On and on he talked. The sounds soothed me, carrying me through the night and through the steady, breathing hills. The land is a listening ear and a singing cradle, Tooth told me, and softly described its song. He had a name for things that leap up unchained, like fear, and another for those that never waver. Fear is a now-and-then smell, he said, but the scent of a dam is always.

I knew every part of what he meant. It was like dream flying, like remembering in your sleep how to do something that came easy once and believing, really believing, that you'd never ever forget the trick again.

How much time passed before I realised he'd stopped walking? I dragged my head up and looked around.

We were in a parking area. The road ended here. To our left I could just make out a low, slab-topped passageway. Through the opening a shimmer flashed.

*Mum.*

I slid down.

'There.'

I remember the walls of the passage pressing around me like slowed-down time. I remember pushing through and stumbling along the path, clutching Tooth's mane for support. I remember the shimmer pulsing like a great bright heartbeat in the dark. I remember huddling against the base of the lighthouse beacon, the cylinder hard against my chest as I sobbed and raged at Mum for leaving me before time.

*You had no business, Mum. No business.*

I remember pleading: *Come back.*

I remember Tooth folding onto his knees.

Then I don't remember.

# 21

At Cape Rēinga the Tasman pushes turquoise against the dark blue Pacific, just like Mrs Pukeroa said. I've seen pictures on the internet. Dad says we'll all go there one of these days for a proper look, but I'm in no hurry.

It took a while for me to get better. By the time the police showed up I was pretty sick – ranting and raving about all kinds of stuff, Dad said, and crying out that Tooth was dead.

They found him near the lighthouse with a bullet lodged between his ribs. He'd stood by me for as long as he could and then lain down. He'd lost a lot of blood. Luckily a police sergeant had horses herself and had known what to do. Her quick thinking saved his life.

The first thing Dylan said when he came to see me in the

hospital was, 'Don't hurt Chewie! I didn't tell for ages and ages!' I had to swear on all my china horses that I wouldn't touch a hair of Chewie's plastic fur head. Then I hugged Dylan so hard he squawked.

Dad patted his shoulder. 'It's true. It was only when Audrey went to the paddock to check everything was all right that we found out Tooth was gone. Dylan hadn't said a thing about the camping gear, so we had no clue you might have gone off on horseback. We all thought . . .' He swallowed and looked away.

'We thought you *drowned*!' said Dylan, his eyes like saucers.

The shame I felt must have shown on my face then. Dad cleared his throat and changed the subject. Later on, when Dylan had gone to get a treat from the snack machine at the end of the ward I blurted, 'I didn't mean for it to be like that, Dad, I swear! When I saw the news I thought we—' I burst into tears. Through the sobs I just managed to say, '. . . I thought we could never come back!'

Dad sat down on the side of the bed and wrapped me in his arms. 'Hey . . . it's all right. It's all right . . .' When my tears finally dried he said, 'You know, this whole thing's my fault more than anyone's. I should have shared my plans with you right from the start. *All* my plans.'

That was when he told me he'd been looking for the right place in Auckland to bury Mum's ashes.

'Once I knew we were moving I couldn't just leave her behind.'

'But I thought . . .' I stopped, confused.

'That I'd forgotten her?'

I nodded. 'You already had Audrey!'

He pulled me close again. Gently, he mussed my hair. 'Oh, Fol, things are never that easy to separate.'

Dylan told them about the pop-up, but it was Ben who tipped the police off about where to find us. And the two Austrian women with their selfie – they'd spotted me and Tooth in a news bulletin a couple of days later and contacted the local police. Patrol cars had driven both ways along the beach looking for us, but it must have been while we were getting lost near the water hole, because they'd missed us. After that the alerts started going out thick and fast – 'If anyone has seen' etc – and they had us in the right place at last. Ben saw our updated pictures on the TV in the campground shop after dinner, cross-checked with his photo of me with Nui, realised Holly was Folly and passed on my coded message. That was when the patrol cars had sped up to the lighthouse.

When I was well enough to answer questions, two police investigators came to see me. One had a lot of nose, the other no hair. In my head I called them Beaky and Cueball.

'Had a win lately?' said Cueball, holding up a crumpled hundred-dollar banknote, the one I'd tried to buy groceries with. The nurses must have found it in my jeans.

I didn't know where to look. Now everyone would know

the truth: I hadn't just let them all think I was dead – I was a thief, too. I stared hard at the bedspread and tried to beam myself out to the hospital carpark, but it was no use; when I looked up again I hadn't even made it to the corridor.

In a small, shaky voice I started telling them how Tooth and I hadn't been able to take the ferry and had stowed away in the camper van instead and seen the bags being dropped off. Then I confessed.

'I stole a lot of money,' I said, my cheeks burning. After a pause I added, 'And a picture out of a library book too.' While I was at it I wanted to get everything off my chest.

When I told them about Mason they traded glances and leaned forward in their chairs. Suddenly they had a lot more questions. I couldn't answer most of them, but they took notes on the stuff I did know. Their mouths sort of quivered when I got to the part about the poo and how that had given us away. Talking about it all brought back the feeling of being chased into the surf and the long ride to the lighthouse. Everything started closing in on me again and I was glad when the ward matron came in and said it was time to rest.

Next day they brought a file of mug shots for me to look at. Ratch was in it, only with a different name. So was one Paul A. Mason.

'Yes, that's him,' I said. He was a bit younger in the photo and he had a small beard, but I would have known those eyes anywhere. 'I cut him on the face with Kiri's keepsake.' The keepsake had fallen out of my hand into the stream, so I drew a picture for them.

Cueball looked at my drawing and pronounced, 'Well the cut won't kill him, but the tetanus might.'

Sergeant Maihi came to see me too. She had a swag of curly black hair and eyes that looked as if she was dying to tell you a good joke. She was still looking after Tooth. He'd been lucky – the vet who'd operated had found the bullet 'about a whisper' from a main artery. The sergeant had put Tooth out to graze with her own horses until we'd both recovered.

'Not shy, is he?' she said the first time we talked. 'Snuck into the barn yesterday and helped himself to my best hay.' She called in regularly to give me updates. 'Aren't you better yet? That pony of yours is a bad influence. He's got the others laughing at me behind my back.'

Mason was working with the big drug gang that had been on the news that day in Rawene when I'd found out everyone thought I was dead. He knew the police were onto him for his dodgy deals and that they were closing in, but the load was too important for him to throw over so he'd come up with the camper van drop idea to get the payment for it through and leave him clean if he got stopped. Then his stooge Ratch had discovered some of the cash was missing and figured out who'd taken it, and the pair of them had come looking for us.

'A farmer who lives near the dunes towed a white SUV out of the stream bed on the night you made it to the Cape,'

Beaky told me. 'Amazing how a bit of quicksand can come in handy, right?' she said with a wink. 'Thanks to your tip-off we caught up with Mason and his crony, but they weren't carrying anything. We couldn't touch them. Then three days ago a police boat unit at the south end of Ninety Mile Beach intercepted some smugglers trying to get away with a pile of dirty money. Payment for a big stash of drugs they'd dropped in a boathouse. Our people are moving in on the load now.'

'The serial number on your hundred note matches other bills they were carrying,' Cueball told me during another visit, 'and some of those connect directly to a very shady banking operation in Mason's name.' He grinned and leaned back in the hospital chair. 'We've been trying to get this fish for quite a while. Thanks to your, ahem, "light fingers" we can link him to the bank shenanigans *and* the drug payment, not to mention the threat to you. The police department is extremely grateful, but let's agree that your life of crime ends here, OK?'

Red-faced, I nodded.

'Phew,' said Beaky, 'the public libraries can breathe again.'

I even had a proper visitor in hospital. Ben came to see me. His mum had driven him up specially from the campground.

He showed me some of the headlines: 'Horse Girl Busts Mr Drugs', 'Ninety Mile Showdown', 'Hoss vs. Boss' – that sort of thing. My favourite was 'Dung Trick Pony'. I couldn't wait to tell Tooth. Ben showed me a video of Mason being led away in handcuffs. There was a line of stitches on his face.

The TV people had been falling over each other to interview me. One channel even wanted to make a documentary retracing the ride Tooth and I had done. The police put out an official statement and advised Dad to 'keep me out of the media circus'. I would have said no anyway. So much had happened – I needed time to think it all through. And it wasn't only about me. Kiri wouldn't thank me if a TV crew suddenly staked out her hut.

Ben was fun. 'When I read your message I thought you were just kidding around. Then I saw your picture on the news.'

He kept forgetting to call me Folly. He asked me about the rest of the ride and promised not to tell any snooping reporters. We even drew a cool map of the route. It was strange to see the whole trip laid out that way, without all the colours and smells and feelings of the road. Or the hours. Maps make it all look way easier.

I trusted Ben. The only thing I kept to myself was the night ride to the lighthouse. That was Tooth's and mine alone. I might never remember the exact sounds he had spoken to me, but their message had gone straight to my soul.

# 22

There's a little cemetery not far from our new place. On one side are the old graves and lurching mossy headstones with letters you can hardly read any more, and on the other are newer plots decorated with rainbow whirlygigs and plastic flower leis and soft toys fading in the sun. Each time I visit Mum I take a different route between the rows and look at some of the names.

It's just as well I never finished my mission at the Cape. Sergeant Maihi told me it's a place to remember the dead, not leave their remains. We buried Mum's ashes near a big tree. I haven't seen her wairua since the ride, so I'm glad there's a place I can go to if something's bothering me and I want to share it with her. A donkey called Chico lives in the paddock next door. Sometimes when I'm talking to Mum he chimes in. Tooth used to say that donkeys are a whole different ballgame, and to hear Chico bray, I can believe it.

I'm going to read the notebook she left me. Not yet – the heart on the cover still reminds me too much of our hug and makes me cry. But soon. Now that I'm done with running away up north I might need some of the things she wanted to tell me.

When I'd gotten over the pneumonia and could leave the hospital, Dad and Audrey drove me to Sergeant Maihi's farm. It's a beautiful place overlooking the sea, with lots of native bush and hills that make you want to ride all over them, exploring.

Tooth was grazing with the other horses. I picked him out from far off, even though he'd put on some weight. He looked right at home. Maybe too much; as I walked towards him over the fields I suddenly had a twinge of worry. What if he didn't want to leave? I'd put him through such a lot – would he refuse to go with me?

He lifted his head and saw me. For a long moment he stood there, just an ordinary-looking bay pony with a longish face and a funny white mark like a tooth. Then he whinnied and broke away. It was a signal; immediately all the other horses cantered after him. The canter became a gallop and soon the whole group was tearing around the field. Tooth bucked and kicked his heels up like a colt. At the far end of the paddock he stopped and reared, hooves pawing at the sky.

I'd never seen him that way. He was different. *But I'm different too. The ride changed us both.*

He moved among the horses, touching noses with them one by one. At last, when he was ready, he came thundering towards the gate, his tail streaming out behind him.

A few paces away he slowed to a trot, blowing and shaking his mane. When I reached out my hand he came forward, sniffing as though he had to get the measure of me all over again.

I flung my arms around his neck. 'I thought—' The rest of the words wouldn't come.

*I thought I'd lost you.*

What had he told me that night? Fear comes and goes, love stays strong. I tried for the hundredth time to remember the horse words but they were out of reach, like a dream.

I started talking about the hospital and Beaky and Cueball, then went on to tell him about Mason and the drug ring. 'And Ben lives in Auckland!'

Tooth said nothing. He was silent as I checked how the bullet wound was healing. He was silent as I put on the halter, and he stayed mute as we walked back to join the others.

'Dad's found a place for you to live,' I said, babbling away, trying to get him interested. 'There's good grazing and a pond and five other horses. One of them's blind. And one's a movie star!'

We were approaching the gate. I could see Dad and Audrey chatting with Sergeant Maihi by the horse trailer. The sergeant said something and Audrey laughed. She still annoyed me, but a tiny bit less. I knew now that Dad hadn't forgotten Mum, like I knew it had been Audrey who'd gone to make sure Tooth was OK when everyone else thought I was trout food. She deserved some credit for that. I'd decided to ease off her a bit.

Tooth still wasn't saying anything. As he ambled along beside me I glanced across, trying to read him. Did a half-lowered ear mean he was fed up with my chatter? Was his swishing tail a good sign or was a fly bothering him? His silence was making me nervous.

'At least you didn't get sent to starvation!' I joked, my laugh sounding brittle and forced.

No reply.

Then it hit me: he wasn't going to answer me – not ever again.

My joy at seeing him again vanished. *You asked too much* – in my mind the knowledge rang as cold and hard as a bell. The secret tie between us had disappeared, lost forever just like the horse sounds that had helped me reach the lighthouse.

Was it true? Had I really used up the special part of our friendship? I thought of all the times during the ride when he'd hinted about turning back. I hadn't listened. Oh sure, I'd *pretended* to ask him what he wanted, but deep down my mind had already been made up to go on. I hadn't even cared enough to realise that he'd been shot.

A chill spread through me. Lose Tooth? Lose the friend I'd poured my heart out to so many times, the one who'd always been there for me and had somehow known just when to make me laugh and when to leave me in peace? He'd listened to my fears during the sad, angry days when Mum had gotten sick and through the lonely months that followed. I remembered the explosion of happiness I'd felt the first time he'd whinnied to see me, the hours spent currying his coat to a shine, our rides together and even his grumpy, pig-headed moments. Losing it all would be unbearable. It would be like going back to riding at Novaks'.

With a heavy heart I took the treat I'd brought him out of my satchel. It was a special surprise – he'd never had strawberries before. After sniffing and blowing and practically snorting one of the fruits up his nostril, he snuffled them off my palm.

I stroked the white marking on his forehead. 'It'll be all right, you'll see. We're going to have lots more good times. We'll—'

I broke off. It wasn't him I had to convince, it was me. Biting my lip not to cry, I looked away and stared at the coast – the *other* coast. Ninety Mile Beach was behind me. Before me lay the rolling Pacific, wide and unknown.

My shoulders slumped. 'What am I going to do?' I whispered.

There was a slurp at my back. I turned. Tooth was standing

there chewing as if he didn't have a care in the world. A trickle of pink strawberry juice was dribbling down his chin. As I watched, still not wanting to accept that everything between us had changed, he swallowed the last berry down and gave a little snort.

'Good start,' he said, nuzzling my arm. 'Does the new place have ryegrass?'

# ACKNOWLEDGEMENTS

I'm fairly certain some galactic alignment was going on the day I found my dream agent, Catherine Pellegrino, whose stellar support has made this journey to print such fun. Similarly, Senior Commissioning Editor Chloe Sackur's wise guidance and sensitive nudging, together with the flair of Jack Noel, Kate Grove and the excellent team at Andersen Press, have brightened every step of the publication process. Sian James, your gorgeous cover illustration makes my heart sing every time.

The list goes on. Writer/manuscript mentor Janice Marriott was definitely the right person under the right sombrero – thank you to Maria Hurley-de Jong for connecting us and for the unflagging encouragement (and work). I had a true ally in Renée Loos, who knows and stands up for the creative heart. Ennio Ranaboldo, ever-generous defender of the literary faith, has always kept the bar as high as it should be and me on my toes to try and reach it.

Miriama Aoake, heartfelt thanks for your insightful perspective. Thanks also to the team at Write Up for the thoughtful feedback, and my gratitude to Alastair G. and Ron T. for those two words. Any cultural missteps are my own.

Some perfectly timed feedback from my online writing pal Matthew Elliott was a godsend (also that fart/sleeping bag ratio). David Green brought beats and Pythagorean zest to the creative pudding. In the early days young super-readers Ruben, Eva, Nina, Matilde, Tessa and Thomas kept turning story pages and let me believe I might actually be getting somewhere, and long before there were any pages at all Davide Gomba just listened, rapt. Everyone de Jong, Fischer, Gordon, Hurley, Oretti, thank you for proving that family love, like the scent of a dam, is always.

Horse farmers Kelvin and Mollie Primmer showed me

incredible hospitality and kindness through my early teens. The lessons I soaked up on their farm are at the heart of this story, seen of course through my 'townie' lens. Sara and Yorick, BFFs, your bond sparked the whole tale.

Bianca, you are my kindred spirit in *pensiero rapido* and a writer's best sounding board. Barnaba, can't thank you enough for kindly and perceptively telling it like it is, no pussyfooting. The emotional touchstone for so many key passages in the book – as in life – has been my sister Renske. And once again to Mauro, who trusts that every kite can fly given a friendly wind, *grazie. Questo è per te.*

# BIRDIE

## J. P. ROSE

Birdie Bagshaw is going to start a new life in the Yorkshire Dales. Yet from her arrival, she is treated like an outsider. When one day the local children's bullying drives Birdie to hide in the nearby coal mine, she's rescued by the last remaining pit pony in the village. As the weeks pass, Birdie forms a special bond with the spirited little pony. But his future is in danger, and Birdie comes up with a daring plan to save his life in return . . .

'A tender and touching story for animal lovers everywhere'
**Hannah Gold**

'A captivating story of the profound and powerful magic of animals'
**A. F. Steadman**

# The HOUSE at the END of the SEA

VICTORIA M. ADAMS

After a family tragedy, Saffi has to move to her grandparents' spooky house by the sea. The walls change colour, a stranger's face appears in the mirror, and she hears eerie music at night. When a party of extraordinary visitors arrive at midnight, Saffi begins to realise that her family has a dark, magical secret.

'Majestic'
**Sinéad O'Hart**

'Delightfully eerie'
**Skye McKenna**

'Brilliant'
**Elen Caldecott**